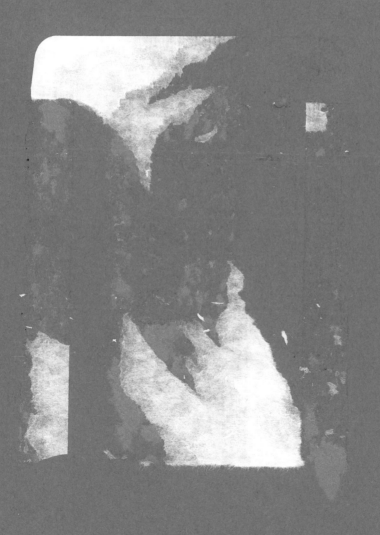

AXEL JOHNSON INC.

HANS DE GEER

AXEL JOHNSON INC.

1920–1995

This book was produced by Bokförlaget Atlantis AB at the request of the author and the Axel Johnson Group. Design and layout were done by Gary Newman on the Macintosh™ computer using Adobe PageMaker™. The type is set in Scandinavian Galliard from Carter & Cone Type Inc. Reproduction work by Digiset AB. Anders F Rönnblom composed the jacket illustration using Live Picture™ on the Macintosh. The paper is 100 gsm woodfree, uncoated Lessebo Linné from Klippanbruken. It is permanent, as well as chlorine and acid-free, thus meeting the environmental criteria for the Scandinavian Swan-mark under license number 304050. Printed and bound by Kristianstads Boktryckeri AB, Kristianstad, Sweden in April 1995.

Axel Johnson Group, Stockholm
Copyright © Text: Hans De Geer
Copyright © Illustrations: as listed on page 273

Produced by Bokförlaget Atlantis AB, Stockholm
Printed in Sweden, 1995
ISBN 91-630-3439-5

Chairman's foreword

THE BOOK you are about to read is the story of Axel Johnson Inc., the American branch of my family's company, which was founded by my great grandfather Axel Johnson. This year Axel Johnson Inc. celebrates its seventy-fifth birthday. To mark this anniversary, a scientific account of the company's history was commissioned a few years ago. This flung us into meticulously organized archives as well as boxes of fading photos, yellowed letters, frayed telegrams and innumerous conversations with people who had once been part of Axel Johnson Inc. You hold the result of our endeavors in your hand.

But, you ask, who cares about company history? Its relevance to Axel Johnson Inc. of 1995, to its fast-moving telecommuncations business or its position in the environmental field must be minimal?

To me, a lack of historical perspective represents a short-sighted view. In the realm of business, as in art, science and even our personal lives, future success has its source in a deep and sincere understanding of who we are today, what driving forces are in place, what strengths and weaknesses we have, and what values and commitments we honor. This understanding of the present requires sharp analysis and even sharper intuition and insight. But describing the present will only provide a superficial understanding of who we are. The present can be truly understood only as part of a continuum that integrates the happenings and values of the past. Thus, our longing and need for a history – its ideas, its events and its people.

In a private company there is a further dimension to our search for understanding – that of its owners and family leaders. The story of Axel Johnson Inc. cannot be distinguished from that of three generations of the Johnson family. The history of the family and the company are intertwined and, in the final analysis, inseparable. I have almost fifty years of memories where family and the business of Axel Johnson Inc. mingle. I recall the late forties when my grandfather and grandmother, Axel and Margaret Ax:son Johnson, visited us in New York to check on the progress and prospects of Axel Johnson Inc. During that visit my grandmother brought me to F.A.O. Schwartz to buy a doll. I recall the early fifties when I dressed up in velvet leggings, a woolen coat and white gloves to pick up my father at his downtown office on Saturday afternoons. Sometimes he seemed worried about business matters, sometimes he was pleased. I recall the sixties when oil distribution and trade required my father's decisions on large investments and risky ventures, and a stream of Axel Johnson Inc. executives invaded our home in Sweden. I recall the seventies when my father increasingly involved me in the business of Axel Johnson Inc., pointing to essentials, guiding and nudging me to see how pieces of the puzzle fit, talking with me about the company's people and operations.

If it were in my hands to dedicate this book to one person, I would dedicate it to my father. Together with my mother, he lived the happiest years of his life in America, building a company of his design. Axel Johnson Inc. is a child of his vision and dreams. He viewed it as a treasure chest to be well guarded, filled with riches to be realized. Many of his dreams came true, but life did not give him full time to complete his task. That assignment is ours and that of coming generations.

VI

This book was suggested by the Swedish historian Hans De Geer, who is working on a larger study of the history of A. Johnson & Co starting in 1873. As a part of this work, he was fascinated by the American-Swedish connection – the people, relationships, failures and successes. He was given full access to all sources and the scientific freedom to question, test hypotheses and draw conclusions. Our cooperation has been constructive and exciting, leading to a fuller understanding of the complexities of building a business and of the people who made it happen.

I hope you will enjoy reading this book as I have.

Antonia Ax:son Johnson

AXEL JOHNSON INC. # Contents

Author's foreword

THE ORIGIN OF THIS BOOK is a research project on the history of the Swedish firm, Axel Johnson AB. What was first conceived of as a chapter in that story has been developed here into a tale of its own, the history of Axel Johnson Inc.

In various ways, I have enjoyed support from different quarters, and I wish to express my appreciation. Antonia Ax:son Johnson and Paul Graf approved of my idea of doing this study, put both archives and financial means at my disposal and encouraged me to follow through. The research project on the Swedish company is supported by The Axel and Margaret Ax:son Johnson Foundation.

I have interviewed many people in connection with my research. Without exception, they all received me graciously, answered my questions and participated in a common effort to investigate the past. Further details on the personal and written sources for this history are given in the References, at the end of the book.

Dr. Axel Norberg, archivist of the Johnson Group, has guided me to the archival sources. Ann-Karin Reuterlöv, of Axel Johnson AB, has planned my travels and aided me in other ways.

The translation of an early version of the manuscript was done by Suzanne Heine, Stockholm, who made it possible for me to communicate my findings to people in the United States. Further research and many discussions led me to considerable additional writing and rewriting of the manuscript before it was put in the hands of Pauline Bilsky, New York, who checked and line-edited the text. With her many years of experience working with Axel Johnson Inc. as a communications consultant, she has greatly contributed not just to the language and style of the text but also to the content of the book, and she has been helpful with illustrations and other practical matters.

An early version of the manuscript was discussed in a seminar at the Institute for Research in Economic History at the Stockholm School of Economics. Professor Ulf Olsson, who chaired the seminar, has also participated in the project in other ways. I am delighted that the book has been accepted for the Institute's series of business history monographs.

It has also been a pleasure to work with the production manager, Lennart Rolf of Atlantis Publishers, the graphic designer Gary Newman, and the illustrator Anders F Rönnblom who together have converted the manuscript into a book, turning the duckling into a swan.

Bromma, Sweden, February 1995

Hans De Geer

The Johnson Building at Stureplan, Stockholm, ➢
the exterior decorated with sculptures by Carl Milles,
has been the headquarters of the Johnson Group since 1919.

New York in the 1920s: the new economic center of the world.

CHAPTER ONE

Introduction

Here is the story of Axel Johnson Inc., an $800 million company with corporate headquarters in Stamford, Connecticut, seven subsidiaries spread all over the United States and business worldwide. The corporation is active in environmental technology, telecommunications, marine engineering, refining of special metals and energy distribution. Its business is a mixture of traditional and modern production. Axel Johnson Inc. is privately held. The owner and chairman of the company is Antonia Ax:son Johnson, a Swedish businesswoman who is also the leader of a Swedish business group with which Axel Johnson Inc. shares most of its history.

The company started in 1920 as a trading office representing the Swedish Johnson Group, then led by the Consul General Axel Ax:son Johnson, grandfather of Antonia. The Consul General's business, inherited from his father, involved him in shipping, steel milling, general trade and later in the interwar years, in construction, oil refining and manufacture, to mention some but certainly not all of his interests. The Johnsons are one of the legendary families in Swedish business history.

The Johnson business started in international trading from a headquarters in Sweden. The Johnson Group's expansion overseas took place in three phases. At about the time of the First World War, trade offices were opened in the most important West-European capitals and in the United States. During the interwar years, offices were also established in South America. In the 1960s, the Group was represented in a wide range of countries in Europe, South Africa and Asia. Of all these ventures, it was the office in New York that developed most forcefully and grew into a diversified industrial corporation in its own right.

Axel Johnson Inc. has existed for 75 years. Longer than the conscious memory of most people. That is one, and presumably the most important reason for *writing* this story: to create an understanding out of human experiences, otherwise lost in the mist of history. But commissioned company histories are not always the most interesting or exciting reading. Realizing that, what reasons can I give you for *reading* this one?

That depends on who you are. Maybe you have worked in the company or in one of its subsidiaries, or in other parts of the Johnson Group? In that case, I hope to refresh your memory, suggest a new framework of understanding, fill in details that you might have forgotten, encourage you to reinterpret your own experience and stimulate your imagination about what just might have happened. Maybe in some respects we disagree; that is unavoidable. You are as entitled to your version of history as I am entitled to mine. We have different sources of knowledge – you have your eyewitness memory and I have archival sources and hearsay from others – and we are likely to have different objectives in our understanding of history. After all, there may be no such thing as *the final truth*. Our disagreement might be the start of a creative process in which we can construct together a set of propositions that we might call *the provisional truth*, that is, the best that we can do for the moment given the various historical evidence.

Maybe you are a business partner, or a prospective business partner, wanting to know more about the company and the people that you deal with? That is a very legitimate option. You want to know who they are, so you ask for the record. Also, Axel Johnson Inc. has a business philosophy, stating the importance that the company places on both tradition and innovation. »As to tradition,« it says in the first paragraph of the document, »we value continuity to build on the Axel Johnson name, position and strength … in the United States and worldwide.« What does that really mean? What is the tradition like, what is the history of the Johnson organization in the United States or worldwide? What business values is the statement referring to, what basic beliefs are demonstrated not just in words but in practice? For you who wish to look underneath the surface of the company code, I want to show this background: There is the Swedish origin, the company's childhood as a tiny trading office in New York, its adolescence as an overseas representative of a big Swedish industrial group and its coming to maturity as a diversified U.S. company at arm's length from the rest of the owner's business-es. I hope to elucidate the formative experiences of this company that give some clues to understanding the identity behind the cor-porate image.

Maybe you are a scholar or a student? In that case, what can this story, or business history as such, add to your knowledge or profes-sional education? I don't know what you are looking for; maybe you are interested in history, economics, administration, organiza-tion theory? There might be something for all. Business history can be written in many different ways, focusing on one aspect or the other, like company growth, organizational change, technological breakthroughs, market performance, financial conditions and re-sults, human resources or labor relations. Business history deals more often with big companies than with small, and often nowa-days scholarly business history uses aggregate statistical data, mak-

The first generations of the Johnson industrial dynasty: Axel Johnson, the founder of the Johnson Group, with his eldest son and successor, Axel Ax:son Johnson, around the turn of the century.

ing a sort of collective business history rather than individual company histories. Illustrated books, published at any appropriate anniversary, about small or mid-sized firms, are often – appropriately – not considered as scholarly works but rather as pieces of eloquent journalism. My ambition, however, is that this book not be classified among those.

In the foreground is the company's growth and corporate strategy, given the transformation from being part of a patriarchally governed conglomerate into being an industrial concern in its own right, and given the differences between the Swedish and the U.S. environment, within which the corporate strategy is formulated. In what sense has the U.S. company been led by the »patriarch« – or »matriarch« – in Stockholm? Has business in the United States developed according to its own American logic, which the Swedish leadership has merely had to accept and adapt to, or have Swedish preconditions determined the liberty of action of the U.S. company? Can anyone sit at a desk in the Group headquarters in Stockholm and in any meaningful sense manage what is going on in a New York office? Is the feeling of being in control a reality or just an illusion? In what way has technological change altered the preconditions, for example change in modes of communication? What impact have changes in international or national institutions had? Have the rules of the game remained stable? Viewed over the long term, has belonging to a Swedish industrial group been a stimulus or a hindrance for the U.S. company in realizing its potential?

So the catchwords for this story could be, for example, management, strategy or the logic of business development. But the story could also be interpreted as an analysis of the internationalization of a national business. You could even say that the basic idea of the Johnson business, started as a trading firm in Stockholm in 1873, survives more genuinely in this U.S. corporation than it does in any entity in Sweden nowadays. It is as if the seed that was planted in New York survives due to more favorable conditions than exist in the environment for the original plant. Scholars who regard the internationalization process as the development of networks have seen this before, how small and rather unimportant nodes in a corporate net gradually gain influence and weight, eventually to take over as the most important actor.

This story could also be perceived as filling in the picture of U.S.–Swedish relations concerning business and trade as well as the transfer of knowledge and innovative approaches. This is a phenomenon with two sides to it, not just the one exploiting the other. The Johnson organization, and others like it, provided an arena for the kind of exchanges that contributed to both U.S. and Swedish economic growth and technological development.

I will not in this context, though, start from or test any specific, clear-cut theory. What I will provide is the story of a single firm. Its very uniqueness is an important asset of this analysis. I am not looking for the most general characteristics, which often are revealed as truisms, nor am I trying to build any basis for generalized statements about the nature of things. Rather, by showing in some detail how Axel Johnson Inc. grew out of the young Swede Gösta Ekström's mission to New York, I will show you what was, in fact, possible under certain circumstances, not what is most likely to happen in any period of time.

This book is a part of a more comprehensive research project on the Johnson Group in Sweden. In the foreground of that study are the problems of management and preservation of ownership over time. Characteristic of the Johnson Group is its nature as a conglomerate, for a long time active in a wide variety of industries. Is it possible, given the level of manufacturing and market expertise that is necessary in contemporary business, to keep such different activities under the control of an active and rather partiarchal management? And, secondly, how can a corporation like that be kept private, in the hands of an active owner? How can the shifts from one generation to another be handled, given the impact of both the repeated partition of inheritance and the toll of taxation? The story of Axel Johnson Inc. also forms part of that wider analysis.

Before we plunge into history, a comment has to be made on the use of names. The Swedish trading firm, from which it all started, was during most of the time called A. Johnson & Co. In 1962, its operations were transferred to A. Johnson & Co HAB, which was changed to Axel Johnson AB in 1988. As a rule, in this text, contemporaneous names are used, and the reader is supposed to interpret them in that way.

Before 1988, Axel Johnson Inc. was called A. Johnson & Co., Inc., which is quite a long name to be used frequently in a narrative text. Other appellations used here are, therefore, expressions like »the American (or the New York) office« for the early days, later, »the New York company«, which is also found in the contemporary (Swedish) company sources. Later still, the U.S. company was regularly called »Inc.« in the Swedish corporate jargon, and the Swedish company was correspondingly called just »HAB« in the American.

Expressions like »the Johnson Group« signify different entities depending on the point in time. Normally this term refers to the sum of owned companies both in Sweden and elsewhere in the world. Most dramatic changes have occured in the Group during the last decade. Nowadays the group of businesses owned by Antonia Ax:son Johnson is referred to as »the Axel Johnson Group«.

In some places, »Johnsons« could be the equivalent of the Johnson Group, while elsewhere it could mean the Johnson family;

the context will tell. The prime actors within the family were first the founder of the firm, Axel Johnson, who lived from 1844 to 1910, and then his son, Axel Ax:son Johnson (1876–1958), often referred to in his lifetime and in this text as »the Consul General«. He was, as his father had been, Siamese Consul General in Sweden. Next was the Consul General's eldest son, who bore the same name as his father and grandfather, Axel Ax:son Johnson (1910–1988). In the Swedish company this Axel was often referred to according to his professional education as »bergsingenjören« (»the mining engineer«); in the American company, he was mostly called »Junior« as long as his father was alive, and after that just »Mr. Johnson«. In this text, the time reference will determine who is Axel Ax:son Johnson: grandfather, father or son. The fourth generation in charge is represented by Mr. Johnson's only child, his daughter Antonia Ax:son Johnson (b. 1943). She is often, in the company as well as in the public arena in Sweden, called just Antonia. In the American company, she is often informally referred to as »Toni«.

It may be worthwhile to reflect a little on how designations have changed. The great grandfather is just called by his name. His son is referred to with an honorary title. In the third generation, the profession designates the person. And in the fourth generation, the head of the family is just called by her first name, »Antonia«. How can that be? Is it a consequence of a growing informalization of society and business life, or is it the modern media's way of referring to celebrities, or is it suggesting a really high position in society? »Antonia« is not a very common name in Sweden, so the risk of misunderstanding is minimal. She just does not need more; she is certainly a media celebrity. Also, with her ladylike appearance and her inherited position, there is no doubt that she is the »queen« of Swedish business society, and royal persons are never called by their family name.

The third and fourth generations: Axel Ax:son Johnson, his wife Antonia and his daughter Antonia (Toni), visiting Japan in the early 1960s.

The disposition of this text is basically chronological, starting around 1900 and ending up with the plans for taking the company into the twenty-first century. Three rather distinct periods can be identified: the interwar years, the three decades 1950–1980, and the period thereafter. These periods roughly correspond to the management of Wilkens, Lynch and Priesing/Anderson/Graf, and there are important differences in scale, scope and strategy among them.

Objectives and strategy are discussed mainly in Chapters 2, 5–6, 12, 14 and 15. Chapters 3–4 take up the different fields of commerce in which the company was active during the early period. Chapter 7 has a similar character, presenting the shipping activity in the middle period. Chapters 8–11 and 13 are devoted to the different lines of business in which Axel Johnson Inc. became involved. They can also, each of them, be seen as »miniature portraits« of the subsidiary companies of the firm: mainly Bird-Johnson, Sprague, Parkson, Axel Johnson Metals, and, representing the »new age«, Hekimian and Larscom. In those chapters, I break the strict chronology by following each of these companies up to 1989, though the corporate development during the 1980s is analysed first in Chapter 12. ADS, which was purchased in 1989 comes into the picture in Chapter 14.

Finally, a remark on the language. In direct quotations the language is reproduced in strict adherence to the source. No modernization is done. This also means that any errors of word usage or spelling or any other kind are not corrected but kept in their original form.

CHAPTER TWO

Incorporation

THROUGHOUT WESTERN EUROPE, the end of the nineteenth century was a time of social and economic change. Industrial society was slowly emerging from the rural past. For individual people, it meant changing their way of living and working, their way of traveling and their way of acquiring information, knowledge and competence.

Around 1900, the population of Sweden was a little over five million. Three out of four people still lived in the countryside. Two out of three earned their livelihood from agriculture. The old rural factory or mill communities (*bruk*), generally devoted to metalworking, forestry and farming, represented a long tradition in Sweden, but their growth potential was no longer as great as it had been. The breakthrough for modern industry, made possible by rationalization in agriculture, really came during the 1870s with the development of the sawmill industry and the revitalizing effect of the Bessemer process on the iron industry, and, ten years or so later, with the development of the chemical pulp industry. Towards the end of the century came the »heroic« age of Swedish engineering, with the founding of one large enterprise after another: L.M. Ericsson, ASEA, AGA, Separator and others. From the 1890s onwards, higher protective tariffs and a growing domestic market also encouraged the development of a consumer goods industry.

Stockholm developed rapidly during the second half of the nineteenth century. Trade and industry flourished. Here Axel Johnson started importing and exporting and, in 1890, founded the shipping company, Nordstjernan, primarily for the Baltic and the North Sea traffic.

In the nineteenth century, Swedish industry was based on substantial foreign trade; the import of capital and the foreign demand for Swedish products made modernization possible. The migration of people and transportation of goods played an increasingly vital role. Most important in this respect was the mighty wave of emigration, which in the course of half a century drove more than a million people from Sweden to the United States. This great stream across the Atlantic implied equally powerful undercurrents locally, regionally and nationally.

The company A. Johnson & Co was founded as a trading enterprise in 1873. It imported coal, coke and chemicals from Germany and England, and exported iron and iron ore to – among other places – Sheffield, which at the time was the hub of the English manufacturing industry. The company was led by the young Axel Johnson, who had acquired his first experience in the business world as an employee of a textile merchant in Stockholm. These were the take-off years of Swedish industry. Thanks to successful investments in the newly established stock market, young Johnson managed to amass the capital necessary to start his own firm. He soon established his trade and worked up good relations in the Swedish as well as the German and British markets. In the 1880s, the firm opened an office in London, but that venture lasted for only a few years.

In 1883, Johnson secured a minority interest in Avesta Iron Works, one of his company's export customers in the Swedish mining region. Avesta was run with varying success until 1905, when Johnson took advantage of an ongoing financial revamping to gain control of a majority of the company's shares. For A. Johnson & Co, this move constituted a fixed investment as well as a large-scale commitment, the consequences of which would substantially influence the entire organization's future development.

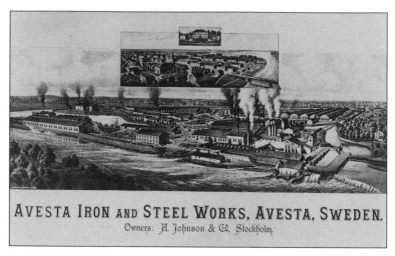

AVESTA IRON AND STEEL WORKS, AVESTA, SWEDEN.
Owners: A. Johnson & Co, Stockholm.

Avesta was an old, rundown steel mill, which Axel Johnson purchased, invested considerable sums in and eventually made profitable.

As early as 1890, Axel Johnson started his second venture: the shipping company AB Nordstjernan, which together with the trading house for many years would constitute the heart and soul of the Johnson Group. Thanks to its overseas expansion, the trading operation soon needed greater shipping capacity, and it seemed only natural to use its own ships. During the 1890s, a number of vessels were bought – primarily for traffic in the North Sea and the Baltic – and the Johnson fleet became a reality.

Maritime affairs came to be of increasing interest to Axel Johnson. For years he nurtured the idea of opening a gateway to Argentina so that Swedish industry in general, and his own company in particular, could take advantage of that market. Johnson took a decisive step in this direction in 1904, when he established a regular shipping line between Sweden and South America's east coast. The shipping company then expanded rapidly. By 1910, when at age 66

At 34 years of age, Axel Ax:son Johnson found himself the head of a growing business group. Strongly supported by his mother, he started his long career as tradesman and industrialist.

Axel Johnson died suddenly of an inflamed appendix and was succeeded in the business by his oldest son, the company had a fleet of eight ships plying regular routes to South America and covering a number of other routes for chartered freight.

A shipping line (Nordstjernan), a trading house (A. Johnson & Co) and an industrial export company (Avesta): Together they comprised a consortium – which we will call here the Johnson Group – at whose helm the 34-year-old Axel Ax:son Johnson found himself. Unlike his father, he had been given an upbringing with an international focus from the very beginning. Some of his early years were spent in English boarding schools, and his language skills were good. At the same time that he succeeded his father as head of the company, he was also appointed to follow him as Siam's Consul General in Sweden. With this appointment, he received the title that he afterwards always preferred, and by which he would be best known: the Consul General.

Characterizing Johnson's management philosophy as patriarchal would be tantamount to understatement. The way in which he dominated his companies seems somehow so self-evident, so much a part of Nature's plan, that it can hardly be called a philosophy at all – if that implies some amount of critical reflection. However, as we shall elaborate later on in this book, management of this kind cannot function as effectively if the distance from which it is exerted becomes too great, or if the patriarch himself becomes incapacitated.

During Consul General Axel Ax:son Johnson's long period at the helm – he died in 1958 – the Group's operations became so diversified that a comprehensive view of the whole is virtually unattainable. Nevertheless, in the most important segments of the picture, it is possible to reconstruct a kind of organic logic underlying the Group's expansion. In the decade after 1910, Johnsons bought mines and made its first inroads into the building and construction sector. During the '20s, Johnsons built a refinery in Nynäshamn, a tiny port on the Baltic. By the 1930s, the Group was acquiring engineering firms; in the 1940s, an insurance company – Sirius – and several communications companies took their place in the Group, most of them acquired through Nordstjernan. We shall not, however, pursue these developments here, but touch upon them when events in our story warrant it.

In the years before and after the First World War, the first phase of the Group's international operation was initiated. Offices were opened in England, France, Germany, Belgium and the United States. Here, our interest will focus on the U.S. office, an affiliate of the original trading company.

The stream of emigrants leaving adverse conditions in Sweden in the hope of a better life in the United States implied also a constant flow of goods, technology and ideas between Sweden and the United States. The traffic was directed via Gothenburg in Sweden or Hamburg in Germany. The export trade between the United States and the Scandinavian countries was of long standing, though for Sweden the most important trading partners were England and Germany. The importation of American farm products to Sweden contributed to the protectionist reaction that surged through Swedish trade policies during the 1880s.

At the same time, several Swedish companies were trying to gain a foothold in the U.S. market. AB Separator had been established in Poughkeepsie, New York, since the 1880s under the name of Lavalco. In 1909, the telephone company L. M. Ericsson opened a sales office in Buffalo, New York, which developed into a manufacturing plant. After some years of good business, the plant was closed down in 1923 due to mismanagement. Sandviken steel mills, the SKF steelworks, the engineering company AGA, and the lumber-and-paper manufacturer Holmen, were also establishing operations in the U.S. market. The growing firm of Axel Johnson, too, early considered to establish itself there. In 1888, Axel Ljungberg made a trip to the United States on behalf of the firm to investigate trade options; however, his trip did not lead to a U.S. presence.

By the end of the century, immigration and industry were aiming at new markets, for example South America. Even though Argen-

Following the stream of emigrants, Johnsons' shipping business expanded. In 1904, the Johnson Line linked Scandinavia to South America. Ten years later, operations were extended to the west coast of both Americas.

tina and Brazil never became serious competitors of the United States as a destination for Swedish emigrants, immigration to those countries held a new fascination for the Swedes. Seen as markets for exported goods, the South American countries – in particular the politically stable Argentina – grew more attractive as the pace of Swedish manufacture of sophisticated engineering products increased. Telephones, lighthouses and milk separators could withstand the competition overseas.

Competition in the shipping industry, as well as cartel formation in the so-called international »conferences«, threw up barriers to block the entry of any newcomers. Realizing that it had been difficult enough to break into the market for South American traffic, Johnson opted at first to give the North American traffic a wide berth. However, events took a new turn towards the end of this century's first decade. Ever since 1907, engineers had been feverishly at work linking the Atlantic with the Pacific via a canal over the Panama isthmus, a canal that would open up the western coasts of North and South America to seagoing traffic, and spare ships the risky, time-consuming voyage around Cape Horn.

In 1909, the elder Axel Johnson was paid a visit by an American businessman named John Rosetter. Rosetter represented the W. R. Grace company, and his visit to Axel Johnson is the first contact known to have been made between Johnsons and Grace. This was a contact that, for several decades, would play a vital role in the Swedish company's activities. W. R. Grace & Co. became a permanent partner, a model and – to some degree – a competitor of the Johnson Group.

W. R. Grace was a family company that traced its history back to the mid-nineteenth century. The firm started as a trading house in Peru, was incorporated in the United States in 1899 and acted as the

In 1914, the Panama canal opened up the American west coast to European shipping lines. The Johnson ship, *Pacific*, was the first non-military vessel to pass westward through the canal.

agent of the Peruvian government for the sale of nitrate of soda. Under the second generation of owners, led by Joseph Grace, business soon expanded in a number of directions: shipping, banking, sugar, cotton and coffee plantations, paper production, tinmining, etc. In the interwar years, Grace went into South American airtransport together with Pan American Airlines and formed Panagra. After World War II, the chemical industry became an important leg of the growing conglomerate, now run by the young J. Peter Grace. During the following decades he developed Grace into a very diversified conglomerate, appearing and disappearing in many different sectors of the economy worldwide. He was of the same generation and became a close friend of Axel Ax:son Johnson Jr., when they met in the American business society of the 1940s.

Back in 1909, the W. R. Grace representative John Rosetter tried to interest Axel Johnson in planning a shipping line through the Panama Canal, the gateway to the West Coast of the Americas. However, Rosetter never got a final answer from the old man. In 1912, though, the Grace company approached Nordstjernan, and two years later, the two companies became partners. The Johnson Line was extended to the Pacific Coast of North America and W. R. Grace, through its San Fransisco office, became Nordstjernan's suppliers and agents there and in the Canal Zone. At that point, Johnson still had no intention of establishing a business in New England or in the New York area.

The outbreak of the First World War in the summer of 1914 fundamentally changed the conditions surrounding trade and shipping in Europe. Although Sweden remained outside the conflict, Swedish business felt the influence of the war, sometimes for the better, sometimes for the worse. The widening of the war zone, the changing conditions in world markets, the increased stringency of political and administrative demands, all made themselves felt.

During the first year of fighting, before embargoes had created serious shortages, the war stimulated Swedish industry. The iron and steel industries, in particular, enjoyed a boom. For the Johnson Group, the times meant good trading opportunities, excellent revenues from shipping and high potential profits from the steelworks in Avesta.

After a few years, the naval warfare grew more intense, not least in the North Sea. Industrial supply from abroad as well as exporting to western markets was becoming more and more hazardous as Sweden became isolated. In December 1915, the Consul General decided to open an office in London under the management of K.V. Mellin. The London office, which was set up as an independent firm, A. Johnson & Co., Ltd., lay outside the immediate war zone; thus it could manage the portion of the Johnson Line fleet that was also outside the war zone and that the Consul General – for a variety of reasons – did not want ordered home. Two employees were dispatched to London to help Mellin, one of whom was a young man, Gösta Ekström. Some years later, Ekström would be appointed to run Johnson's first office in New York.

In 1917, Germany declared total submarine war, which in due time led to the United States' involvement in the conflict. At first, the British parried by tightening their blockade of the German harbors. The British forced neutral ships into port at Kirkwall, on the Orkney Islands, to be inspected for contraband. Things were no different in the United States, where federal officials subjected all incoming vessels to rigorous inspection, especially the neutral ones.

These circumstances undermined any chance Johnson may have had of managing his ships solely from London. Hostilities were now taking place in the Atlantic Ocean, and Johnsons had to move further west to find room to maneuver. In April of 1917, Mellin was ordered to send Gösta Ekström to New York to set up an office that would serve both as the Johnson Line's agents and as the supply office for its fleet. Ekström was also assigned to try to influence the U.S. government to carry out inspections in Halifax so that ships would not have to take the long detour by way of Kirkwall. From the office in New York – which, although it was Johnsons' de facto branch office, was formally registered as a private firm in Ekström's name – Ekström made his reports to London.

In September 1910, as a young man just starting out, Gustaf E. (Gösta) Ekström found employment with A. Johnson & Co. He was the son of Captain John Ekström, who worked for the Johnson shipping line between 1905 and 1925. In Sweden, young Ekström had specialized in steel exports, and it was thanks to his expertise in this field that he had been sent to London in 1916. The Consul General wanted the office in New York to help provide Avesta and the rest of the trading organization with investments. To this end, he especially impressed on Ekström the necessity of getting licenses for the export of ferromanganese.

The office in New York soon received new assignments. From August 1917 on, an embargo on all trade with neutral states was in force in the United States. In the autumn, the newly elected liberal government in Sweden initiated trade negotiations with the United States as a first step towards improving relations between neutral Sweden and the Western Allies. The news filled Ekström with enthusiasm. He now felt that there were no limits to the New York office's potential, and he set about drawing up plans at once. He would transform the New York office into a more independent and active unit. Maybe the federal trade policies could be influenced in order to secure special treatment for the Johnson fleet? If not, and if it was impossible to export to Sweden, then the company would ship its exports where it could, for example to South Africa. He

26

would open an agency in South America. Even Russia – which between the revolutions of March and October 1917 was perceived as a liberated country by the Americans – looked like a promising market.

When the war ended in late 1918, the commercial world began gearing up for the return to a state of peace. But it would take time. Companies had to adapt themselves to different conditions in newly opened markets and orient themselves to new competition. In the summer of 1919, plans began to crystallize for transforming Johnson's office in New York into a full-fledged American affiliate. During that summer, Ekström was in Europe. He represented A. Johnson & Co in Poland, where iron ore and coal were the topics of discussion. Plans were made for the New York office's renewed participation once direct trade between »Free Europe« and America got under way. However, that meant that a fully clear legal position would have to be worked out for the American office.

Ekström realized that the office would have to be listed as a company in the commercial register of some American state. An incorporation would guarantee that the rest of the Johnson Group would not be responsible in a fiscal or legal sense for what was done in the United States. In August 1919, Ekström wrote to the Consul General to say that a method of organizing had already been looked into by a pair of lawyers, Dean and Cravath. At the same time he promised to present suggestions for putting together a board of directors.

In September Ekström, hurrying back to the United States (in part, to avoid military service in Sweden), found out that the Consul General had negotiated with one Colonel Edward G. Robinette, who had agreed to serve as a director of the proposed company. Johnson had previously employed Robinette as his advisor on questions concerning federal regulations and the sale of coal. Now Robinette, too, was on his way back to the United States, armed with Johnson's authorization to take up negotiations with the U.S. Government, something that Ekström was instructed to facilitate in every way. Johnson explained the advantages of the arrangement:

> [so that we] ... on our Board get the advice and assistance of a person who is also very confident with things and matters over on this side. Besides, through the long acquaintance I have with Mr. Robinette, I can at the same time have full confidence in him.

Robinette's appointment to the board ensured that the company had someone in its ranks who possessed knowledge of how the American establishment worked, as well as personal contacts with its movers and shakers. But relations between Robinette and Ekström were not without friction. Ekström often felt slighted by the authority vested in Robinette by the Consul General, especially in view of Robinette's penchant for acting somewhat aside from the interests of the New York office. Robinette had become Axel Ax:son Johnson's de facto emissary, quite outside of the formal management hierarchy. This way of steering operations, which was to become Johnson's common practice, in the long run led to a great many problems. In the opinion of Curt Benckert, Johnsons' chief treasurer, voiced in a letter to the Consul General, all business activities should instead have been conducted through the office itself.

Benckert had arrived in the United States in the autumn of 1919 to study modern business methods and office organization as they were practiced at W. R. Grace & Co. There he was allowed to see the bookkeeping, which did not appear very technically advanced, but he was never made privy to the records of Grace's trading departments, which represented the company's strength. The files were confidential, and no outsiders, however trusted business partners

A. Johnson & Co., Inc., was incorporated in Delaware in 1920. »Delaware is a state where a great many incorporations are filed and organized. That is a very favourable state for corporations and especially those who seek to sell stock in the financial centers of the United States«, reported a San Francisco lawyer to the Consul General. Other options discussed included Maine, Nevada and New York.

they might be, were at liberty to peruse them. Now, Benckert was assigned to participate in the preparations for forming the new Johnson corporation. Under his supervision, and with the help of Philip Dean, a lawyer who would act as Johnson's U.S. legal advisor for many years, registration of the company took place in Delaware on March 11, 1920.

Registering the company in Delaware was a practical move; the state's laws were considered to favor business. The formal founders of the company were Benckert, Ekström, Robinette and Ernst Rosengren, an energy expert sent out from Stockholm in 1919 to improve the U.S. office's coal business and to study how oil could be used in industrial processes so that he would later be able to manage oil deals from Sweden.

Ekström, Robinette and Rosengren were voted in as directors. Ekström was chosen to serve as president, and Theodore Alm was appointed secretary and treasurer. He had been one of Ekström's closest aides since 1917; in the summer of 1920, he was obliged to request reassignment to Sweden because of illness.

A number of alternative configurations were considered before the Board of Directors was finally put together. Proceeding from the premise that Johnson was starting the company to have a safe place to invest money, Robinette suggested that the board be made up of prominent persons in the world of finance. Ekström's suggestion, a board made up of businessmen from outside the company, was intended to provide the company with business competence and market contacts. The third alternative – the one that was finally adopted – consisted of naming a nominal board made up of the company's employees, who could be replaced when the Consul General's plans crystallized, perhaps as the result of his visiting New York in person.

The company's capital stock was declared at $100,000, a sum under the control of A. Johnson & Co in Stockholm. Four share certificates containing 250 shares each were made out to the four founders, who endorsed the certificates in blank so that they could be turned over to the Swedish company, A. Johnson & Co, at any time. Formally, neither the Consul General nor any member of his family were shareholders or functionaries in the new company.

The principal reason for transforming the office in New York into a corporation was to make it possible to do business in the United States with limited financial responsibility and without the risk of any investigation by U.S. authorities into the affairs of the Swedish company. But there was also an urgent reason. In February 1920,

Ekström got orders to make all due haste. The reason – still not fully corroborated, however – may have been the potential opportunity to buy surplus warships from the U.S. Government, which Johnson mentioned in a January 1920 letter. The qualifications for taking advantage of these sales were laid down in the American Merchant Marine Act, which stipulated that surplus war vessels could be sold, through the U.S. Shipping Board, only to American citizens. Can that be why the Consul General in a February letter said that incorporation could not wait?

The office in New York was the Johnson Line's formal agent on the East Coast of the United States. In that position, it was responsible for arranging freight shipments. One issue that took a good deal of time and effort concerned a suit that Johnson filed against the U.S. government over two ships, the *Pacific* and the *Kronprins Gustaf*. The ships had been detained during the war by U.S. Federal authorities in an attempt to pressure neutral Sweden. These legal proceedings advanced at such a snail's pace that a settlement was not reached until well into the 1930s.

By establishing an outpost in New York, Axel Ax:son Johnson was trying to gain a foothold for his traditional business in the promising and challenging U.S. market. »I believe that we should concentrate on iron, oils and chemicals, and coal, which are indeed the products we have always dealt with,« he wrote to Ekström in the beginning of March 1921. Together they strived to build up the competence of the New York office. In 1920, an expert on steel joined Rosengren, the oil expert who had come the year before. Ekström's firm optimism was shared at the headquarters in Stockholm.

In the latter part of 1920 and throughout 1921, however, the financial situation in Sweden was turning sour. Axel Ax:son Johnson started to inundate his man in New York with tips about markets to pursue and people to contact. In January 1920, he mentioned alternatives for marketing a diesel motor that had been improved by Nordstjernan's chief engineer. In November, he touched on the idea of doing currency deals and discussed financial operations with the company's lawyers. Meanwhile, Ekström aquired, on his own, an agency for Svenska Tobaksbolaget (the Swedish Tobacco Company), giving the company a modest but steady income.

The post-war depression hit the Swedish economy hard, not least the iron and steel industries in which the Johnson Group had a large portion of its investments. The Group's very survival was at stake in the financial turmoil. Farsighted strategy gave way to the necessities of the near term. All forces in the Group had to join in order to avoid the divesting of Avesta. In May 1921, Ekström was urged to do all he could to sell Swedish iron and steel in the United States, and in June, the Consul General ordered that drilling steel be imported from Avesta. »The most important thing is that we are able to keep Avesta going, and to that purpose a good many orders will be needed, which, I hope, you will succeed in getting,« wrote Johnson to Ekström in the autumn of 1921.

The crisis forced the Consul General into implementing drastic plans to sell off all kinds of other assets. He was even willing to sell property in the Swedish mining region to repatriated Swedish-Americans, and was anxious to get in touch with American coin collectors about selling his own collection (which now is to be seen at the Coin Museum in Avesta). Ekström was called on to sell parts of Nordstjernan's fleet. Negotiations were undertaken with the Dollar family of San Francisco, but no deals were made. Instead, Johnson's entire steamship fleet was sold to the German shipping company of Hugo Stinnes, and Nordstjernan switched completely to diesel-driven ships.

During these first years, the coal trade exposed two weaknesses in Johnson's concept for his American business: the question of the office's sole right to do business in the U.S. market and the question of how profits should be shared between different parts of the Johnson Group. Import of American coal to Sweden after the First World War had become difficult due to U.S. export regulations. In practice, these amounted to a coal embargo since export involved great business risks. Against the New York company's advice, the Gothenburg office of A. Johnson & Co entered into such an uncertain deal. Robinette, the coal expert hired by the Consul General and a director of the New York company, emphasized the importance of working via the New York office and not trying to deal directly with the U.S. market. During autumn 1920, regulations became somewhat easier, and deals were closed between the New York office and other units of the Group. Ekström argued that his company should get its share of the profits, but the Consul General turned a deaf ear and all profits went to Stockholm. Controversies over this and other matters that arose between the company in Sweden and the office in New York were to become an incessant source of irritation in the future, not least in connection with oil trading.

The optimism that Ekström felt in the beginning hardened into pessimism and the friction between Ekström and Johnson burgeoned into distrust. Ekström felt mistreated and his position was unclear. He looked for more independence and economic resources. He wanted to pursue a career on his own and in the beginning of February 1923 he wrote to Johnson:

[I] have concluded from your attitude that you are not desirous of my future advancement within your Head Office. When I consented to continue here after war it was on your assurance no other's, and on your urgent request. – Notwithstanding fact that I should thus work for Head Office interest and done so faithfully, such work has not been recognised, but has been judged entirely by nett [sic] result New York Office books, whose profits nevertheless has been fixed by Head Office and frequent complaints have been made based on result. On account thereof find it now necessary lay foundation independent career. Much regret must ask you relieve me of present duties on your behalf from 1st of April. Intend to generally continue present activity …

Ekström left in April 1923, taking with him the Swedish Tobacco Company agency. Optimistically he started his own agency in New York soon thereafter. However, luck was not with him for very long. In 1926, Gösta Ekström shot himself in his office.

CHAPTER THREE

Selling steel for Avesta

A REORGANIZATION of the business was clearly necessary; Ekström's purchasing office was shut down in April 1923. By May a new office was opened with the marketing of Swedish industrial products in the United States as its primary assignment. This did not imply any major change, however; the idea was to make the New York office »a paying concern«. A new president was sought, and the job went to Leo W. Wilkens. During his 22 years in that position, a remarkable and not always happy interplay developed between the management in New York, the Consul General and the other companies in the Johnson Group. Actually, the goal of earning a profit was never achieved during Wilkens' time, and the reasons for that were many, as we shall see.

Wilkens was born in 1894. He came from Malmö, a town in southern Sweden, where his father had run a business. Young Wilkens left Sweden in 1915 to work in international trade. He had been employed by W. R. Grace in San Francisco, most recently as its No. 2 man in Shanghai. During a visit to Sweden in 1921, Wilkens had met the Consul General and discussed developments on America's west coast. In a letter dated January 1922, he suggested taking over the agency for the Johnson Line from Grace in San Francisco – his model was Ekström in New York. The import of Swedish paper and pulp would provide, along with the agency, a sound basis for

Son of a Swedish tradesman,
the 29-year-old, internationally experienced
Leo W. Wilkens took charge as president of the New York office in 1923.

business. The Consul General replied frostily that he did not contemplate making any changes in his American representation. But when he looked for a new manager for New York, Wilkens' name came up through the Swedish Consul in San Francisco, Carl Edvard Wallerstedt, for whom Wilkens had done some work.

Wilkens took over as manager of the New York company on April 1, 1923. Curt Benckert remained a director, together with

Stoddard B. Colby of the law firm Dean, King & Smith. The new office was set up in the Whitehall Building on Battery Place. In a telegram to Benckert, Johnson confirmed an appointment on trial and reserved the right to engage an experienced »steel man« as co-director. Obviously he did not trust Wilkens as a representative for Avesta. He wrote to Wilkens on his duties:

> ... at the same time that you take charge of our interests in New York and on North America's east coast, and try to cultivate our connections there, we request that you also turn your attention to business of North America's west coast. As ... pointed out, we are especially keen on developing a market for Avesta's special steel, drilling steel, tool steel, billets and blooms, and we feel that considerable trade in crude bars, pig iron and ferrosilicon is within reach. We request that you keep the office's expenses down as far as possible, and we hope that you will keep us up to date on the progress of the New York office's work.

The company's assignment was to take care of the Johnson Group's interests. During the interwar years, the Group in Sweden moved into a great many new fields – among them, engineering, construction, oil and manufacturing. The New York company was obliged to carry on to the best of its abilities, even on new and unfamiliar ground. Apart from the most important of its assignments, namely to trade for Avesta, a variety of ideas were tested in the attempt to develop a profitable business in the office.

The office was constantly asked to market different kinds of general merchandise as a means of seizing every opportunity to better its consistently bad financial results. As time passed without the New York company showing a profit, the Consul General began to be annoyed. In the spring of 1926, he wrote to Wilkens:

We do not keep the New York office solely for our amusement, the intention is for it – at least in the beginning – to pay for itself and cover its own costs … There must be a substantial weekly profit to meet expenses, and I hope to see as soon as possible the diversion of the office into this direction. The office in New York has now been in operation since 1917, and no other office has had to work so long to reach a result that enabled the office in question to support itself; for with as many different wares as the company's various departments processes in different places, an office need not be run at a loss.

In a similar position, Ekström had got hold of the agency for the Swedish Tobacco Company, and it was urgent that Wilkens find something. Earlier Wilkens had planned to sell Swedish paper and paper pulp in the United States. He tried in vain to take over the Holmen Manufacturing's newspaper agency. In March 1925, he again attempted to get a paper deal going. A certain sluggishness – which frequently characterized the decision-making process at the main office in Stockholm – caused the whole thing to peter out.

But the distant creativity in Stockholm was impressing. The very diversity of the requests would drive Wilkens to despair. For example, in one and the same letter the Counsul General could request information about American methods used in mortar manufacturing, order an investigation of the prospects for exporting stainless steel, and urge Wilkens to leave no stone unturned to facilitate the Swedish Crown Prince's impending visit to the United States. A number of different business ventures were tried with various results: shipping bananas, selling sand to U.S. glassworks, selling pig iron, dealing in borax for the Hamburg office, selling cement to South America, procuring orders for ships for Swedish shipyards, importing timber and exploiting peat in Canada.

But, Wilkens pointed out, working with first this, then that was not possible in the U.S. market, where real factual knowledge was needed in each area. He suggested that a thorough evaluation be done of how business could be developed not just between the parent company in Stockholm and its New York offshoot, but also with the sister companies in Europe and South America. The first venture was selling insulating paper in cooperation with the London office, but the market was sluggish. In collaboration with the Hamburg office, the New York company sold beer barrels; and nickel ore, ferrochromium and other businesses were looked into now and again.

Wilkens was also buying stock for the Consul General. That was hardly risk-free, and Johnson had his doubts about Wilkens's competence in the field. The investment was not particularly extensive, which was noted with a certain satisfaction when the stock market crashed in October 1929. Throughout the 1930s, Wilkens would continue to give the Consul General advice on how to invest his money in the New York stock market. Real estate also came into the picture. A building was bought in New York. The deal was effected in partnership with the lawyer Philip Dean. The building was sold in the autumn of 1929 at a good profit and another property, a 1,200-acre piece of land called Black Pond in Putnam County, some 130 miles from New York City, was bought instead.

From the beginning, by far the most important task for the New York company was to sell steel from Avesta on the U.S. market. During the First World War, when demand for steel products was strong, Johnson had »integrated backwards«, securing Avesta's supply of raw materials by buying iron mines and a blast furnace. The assignment to the New York office can be seen as an integration forwards, a market investment to safeguard an earlier investment in

Engelsberg, an old blast-furnace and forge about 110 miles west of Stockholm, was purchased by Johnsons in 1916 in order to secure iron and
charcoal deliveries for Avesta during the steel boom of the First World
War. Operations were ended in the early '20s. In the 1960s, the old barn
was converted into a modern central archive for the Johnson Group,
housing also the main source material for this history. In 1993, Engelsberg with its manor and other old buildings was put on UNESCO's World
Heritage List in recognition of its unique character.

production capacity. The United States was a vast and important
potential market. Swedish iron and steel were traditionally exported there either through independent trading houses or by the
different sales organizations of the iron works and steel mills. In
addition to distributing Avesta's products, the New York office was
assigned to buy machinery and to snap up new ideas on the production and processing fronts.

In the beginning of the 1920s, the Swedish steel industry was in a crisis, aggravated by structural flaws that had been apparent even before the war and were intensified by the damage that the war inflicted on the international markets: import competition, overcapacity, falling prices, staggering debts and rising labor costs. Men of the trade in Sweden saw one of two ways out of the crisis: to establish a cartel powerful enough to drive up prices in the export markets, or to pare down production and make it more efficient. The cartel option was the first to awake a response from the industry – U.S. Steel and Bethlehem Steel were named as models – but a cartel could only be effective if the number of its members was kept at a minimum. In due time, these plans led to a merger that resulted in the creation of Fagerstabruken AB (the Fagersta Works Inc.) in 1926. To market its products, a special company was set up, Brukskoncernens Försäljnings AB (later, Brukskoncernen AB), and it was represented in the U.S. market by the Swedish Steel Mills American Agency, Inc., which had represented Fagersta earlier. Sandviken's Iron Works had also been well-established in the U.S. market for some years, largely through its own sales organization. The products these companies exported varied in nature, but they all competed with Avesta in that company's most vital areas.

The Consul General had no intention of letting Avesta be part of a cartel, nor even of cooperating with one. On the other hand, he was no stranger to the idea of acting as an agent for Swedish companies other than his own. In one letter to Ekström, he had expressed his regrets that the New York office did not land the agency for Gränges in the United States and Canada, as it would have been a profitable deal.

In the years between the wars, serving Avesta's interest turned out to be no easy job. Avesta had technical knowledge and the New York company had marketing know-how, but the two entities generally communicated through their common owner, the Consul General. This arrangement would prove to be a long, drawn-out triangular drama that never achieved even a modicum of harmony. Wilkens' problems were great. First of all, he had no technical training and lacked the necessary competence with regard to steel; thus the plan from the beginning was to take on an assistant director. Second, the U.S. market was hard. The economy was pressed and competition for the few orders that came in was fierce – not least from other Swedish steelmakers. Third, Wilkens did not have great enough resources to build up a sales organization commensurate with the demands of the market. Thus, the U.S. company did not show a profit, but remained constantly dependent on resources from Sweden, which was not easy considering the Johnson Group's precarious financial situation in the early 1920s.

One of Wilkens' first actions was to employ a more knowledgeable »steel man«, and he came up with Harvey Harding. This was a choice that would prove to be both a stroke of good fortune and a source of enduring irritation. Harding made his mark on Avesta in three specific contexts: plans for a joint venture with U.S. Steel concerning carbon steel, the marketing of drilling steel and licenses for stainless steel.

The first of these ventures concerned grandiose plans drawn up in the summer of 1924 to come to an agreement with U.S. Steel for the export of carbon steel. This deal, which was to be financed by the American steel giant, would have involved a dramatic expansion of the facilities in Avesta, making it the largest steel works in Sweden. Wilkens was enthusiastic, as was the Consul General; but managers in Avesta were considerably more sceptical. If these plans became reality, they argued, Avesta could very well become dependent on – not to say directed from – the United States. Harding visited Avesta in April 1924 and returned in July with a technician from

Avesta, an old town once famous for its copper production, with a steel mill, saw mill, and hydropower station as well as an old manor house close to the town church, became not only the Consul General's favorite company but also the place where he preferred to spend his weekends.

U.S. Steel. After that, however, nothing more was heard about this lofty scheme.

The second context in which Harding was to figure prominently concerned the marketing of Avesta's drilling steel. This was to be one of the New York company's most prolonged business deals. Sandviken, another Swedish steel mill operating in the U.S. market, was a tough competitor in drilling steel thanks to its contract with Ingersoll Rand, the dominant steel marketer in America. Through Harding, the New York company was put in contact with the second largest company, the Chicago Pneumatic Tool Company (CPT), with the purpose of establishing a relationship similar to the one between Sandviken and Ingersoll, which the Consul General interpreted thus:

> Ingersoll have to send in orders continuously, whether corresponding quanitites sold or not, and have undertaken to keep sufficient stocks at the most important places ... all risks, costs and charges falling on them ... They always gets offers, valid until withdrawn, in Swedish Kronor free Sandviken or f.o.b. Gothenburg ... payment to be effected cash against documents in New York according to shipments made, whether lots shipped have been sold or intended for some stock. As regards the consignment lots, they have then, of course, on the other hand, also the advantage to buy at Sandviken's general price, whilst their selling prices are as a whole sufficiently increased to cover not only the expenses and their usual profit – calculated to be 10% – but also an increased profit. According to my opinion about the most advantageous arrangement for both parties concerned ...

Johnson was now prepared to entrust CPT with the exclusive U.S. agency for Avesta's drilling steel on the condition that they bind themselves to push Avesta steel exclusively on the U.S. market. The deal was to be closed directly between CPT, the New York company and Avesta. Johnson left Wilkens some negotiating leeway but only with regard to terms of payment and estimates. However, it was impossible for Wilkens to arrive at any agreement with CPT in view of the strict conditions that the Consul General had stipulated; competition from other manufacturers was too great. He had to close a less favorable deal. As soon as Avesta had been stabilized in the market, prices and conditions would be adjusted in the right direction, Wilkens assured his boss.

It was difficult for Avesta to manage both the quantity and the quality of steel that CPT demanded. When a consignment of drilling steel sent to CPT was found to be inferior, Avesta's technical manager, Walfrid Eriksson, was sent to America. Tests were made and attempts carried out to reprocess the steel on the spot, but the process was slow. CPT could not sell the consignment, while Avesta and the Consul General insisted that it be sold before a new consignment could be shipped. The situation developed into a »Catch-22«, which also undermined confidence between the New York company and the Consul General. Harding's reputation as a very good »steel man« was beginning to erode.

At the same time, the stainless steel market was rapidly and profoundly changing, and there Harding found the opportunity to make his third contribution to the development of Avesta's business in America. Stainless steel had been developed in English and German laboratories during the First World War and already been put to some limited use. English stainless was patented in Sweden in 1918, and used since 1922 in, for example, the manufacture of cutlery.

A Swedish competitor, Fagersta, had started, under the English patent, to produce temperable stainless steel that could be honed. Avesta had fallen behind. Some research had been carried out, but discontinued in 1921 for financial reasons. Now Avesta's plant managers got in touch with the leading European firms, Firth Brearly in Sheffield and the Krupp works in Germany. The result was that in spite of the economic crisis, a small electric steel furnace was installed at Avesta to produce stainless steel. The demand was there, the Consul General believed.

The patent for stainless steel was held by the Firth Brearly Stainless Steel Syndicate. It was so narrowly defined that it could not prevent other manufacturers from producing similar alloys, nor from exporting them to the most important markets in Europe. For this reason, Axel Wahlberg, chairman of the Swedish Ironmasters' Association, after conferring with a number of Swedish steel manufacturers (Johnson was not among them), had refused an offer to purchase manufacturing licenses from Firth Brearly. In the meantime, the American Stainless Steel Corporation (ASS), which had manufacturing rights in the United States, brought suit in 1923 against another company for patent rights infringement. By autumn 1924, it was clear that ASS had won and it would be necessary to purchase licenses from them in order to export stainless steel to the U.S. market. In 1924, a cooperation agreement between Firth Brearly and Krupp locked the European markets shut. Now, Johnson and Avesta had gained the advantage.

By establishing contacts with ASS and various U.S. buyers of stainless steel, Harding made a connection with Firth Brearly. In the contract he reached, Avesta recognized Firth Brearly's patent and received the export license for the United States. In return, Avesta would relinquish the English and German markets. This agreement reflected Firth Brearly's confidence in Harding and his assessment of the demand in the United States.

In the negotiations, Harding used a statement from ASS recommending that he personally be given the sole right to import Swedish stainless steel to the United States. This statement also gave him an advantageous position in negotiations with Avesta and Johnsons. He demanded to be made president of the New York company. If not, he threatened, he would open his own firm and begin importing steel, sidestepping A. Johnson & Co., Inc. (See also Chapter 5.)

Step by step, the old mill at Avesta was modernized. The way out of the
steel crisis of the early 1920s was a new product line, stainless steel. An
electric induction furnace, better adapted to melting stainless steel than
other furnaces, was installed in the middle of the 1930s.

In light of this, and remembering the drilling-steel difficulties with CPT, we can understand the Consul General's letter to the New York company in July 1925, written after finding out that Fagersta was still selling steel in the United States. He wrote:

> When hearing of all this it is very unsatisfying to know that we are not selling any steel and that we are laying with a very big stock in New York, which we do not get rid of ... All these people get cash payment and do not have this credit-system, which also has proved unsatisfactory. In this letter I do not want to get into the matter of stainless. I am very dissatisfied with the way mr Harding has handled this business against my instructions. Still to-day I do not know anything about the contract he signed, although he promised me to place everything before me in cable, in case it should prove necessary to sign before sending the contract for approval here. I do not stand any kind of nonsense. My New York office shall sell the steel and the rustless shall also be combined with this office. Should the contract not prove to be in accordance with my instructions, I have no interest in this contract at all. ... If I find that personal interests are placed before my interests then I am absolute impossible to move one way or another.

Howard Harding began to seem untrustworthy. Earlier Wilkens had characterized Harding as »a very good 'outdoor steelman'«, but in a September 1925 letter to the Consul General, he labeled him a »very expensive but substantially useless person«, who delayed and stalled progress, besides compromising the company's good name at every turn. The conflict between Harding and the factions opposing him was never resolved. Harding died suddenly on September 30, 1925.

Two years have been lost, Wilkens said as he took a new tack in the autumn of 1925, suggesting that the task of entering the U.S. steel market would not be easy. The Consul General and his man in New York were still not in accord about a suitable market strategy and past events had left both parties with a basic mistrust. Johnson was eager for results from the agreement with CPT about drilling steel. As far as other Avesta products were concerned, he wanted a network of agents who could take orders for direct sales f.o.b. Gothenburg while receiving cash payment against documents in New York.

For Wilkens the most important thing was to establish Avesta in the U.S. market. Avesta's prices were too high, and Ingersoll Rand, the prime competitor, had been established in the market for over ten years. Avesta must be able to deliver c.i.f. New York, and the mills had to be able to satisfy trial orders quickly. Stores of merchandise should be stocked in certain cities, perhaps under Avesta's own supervision, to intensify its market presence. Avesta would have to bear the increased costs of stockpiling over the long term. On this basis, a network of subagents could be organized, Wilkens thought, and he tried to do this in Detroit, Chicago and Canada.

But the managers at Avesta objected to Wilkens' plans. They would depress Avesta's prices even further. Wilkens maintained that this strategy was the only course open and that the investment would pay off in the future. The argument that Avesta was not maintaining high enough quality was difficult for the Consul General to accept. He was indeed selling well enough in other places! And as far as stockpiles were concerned, it was enough to have them on two locations! But Wilkens was adamant: In tests carried out in the United States, Avesta had come only third. And to have warehouses on just two locations in the United States would undermine the whole strategy and be a declaration of no confidence. Johnson

Walfrid Eriksson, here portrayed by Helmer MasOlle, was plant manager at Avesta from 1927 to 1949. He became a good friend of Leo Wilkens during long stays in the United States in the 1920s.

was not at a loss for an answer. The problem, he felt, was not in manufacturing, but in the sales organization. He would send Walfrid Eriksson to the United States together with Gösta Lindström, the sales manager, to study the market and evaluate alternative strategies.

Wilkens was delighted to have Walfrid Eriksson come to New York. He held him in high regard as a person and he needed his technical competence. Wilkens' relation to Gösta Lindström was of another stripe: Lindström had been very sceptical of Wilkens' management capability. But after assessing the situation on the spot, Lindström committed himself wholeheartedly to Wilkens' strategy. Competition had intensified dramatically between the European suppliers, and domestic U.S. production had improved in quality. Customers' demand for safe and timely deliveries had become so great that direct ordering of a standard range of goods from across the Atlantic was no longer feasible. It would be absolutely necessary for Avesta, at its own expense, to open a number of warehouses. Wilkens' plan was sound, Lindström reported to the Consul General. Whether or not Avesta had the resources to carry it out was another matter.

Wilkens was allowed to proceed. Warehouses were built in a number of locations, but the Consul General was still sceptical. He traveled in the United States in the late winter of 1927. In a letter to Wilkens, he complained that the warehouse agents he visited had never been able to show him any major orders. Business was slow. New complaints about the quality of the steel came in, and the long wait for laboratory testing brought things almost to a standstill. By the beginning of summer 1927, the tests were shown to be in Avesta's favor. But by late autumn, problems still remained. Avesta's prices were too high. It had limited laboratory resources, its products were not adapted to customer needs – it used European dimensions even in the U.S. market – and its service was poor.

The fact that Wilkens learned more and more about steel and that Walfrid Eriksson (who became plant manager at Avesta in 1927) had spent such a long time in America should have appreciably improved collaboration between the manufacturers in Avesta and the sales organization in New York, and it should also have improved Avesta's ability to adapt to the U.S. market. This, however, was not the case. The problem with CPT and the drilling steel continued to rankle.

As far as stainless steel was concerned, Avesta first extended its production capacity towards the end of the '20s, and again in several stages during the '30s. But its market performance in the United States did not improve comparably. Consignments were faulty, deliveries were late, quality was uneven. Under such circumstances, good sales work was hard to achieve, Wilkens explained in a letter:

> It develops more clearly, as further complaints come in, that Avesta has been unpardonably careless in the execution of their late shipment to this country ... Avesta's attitude and policy, as well as their laxness in execution of orders, has again very much upset me, especially as I am convinced that if Avesta would permit us to operate on a competitive basis and give us sound material we would in a comparatively short time be doing a satisfactory business for them as for ourselves ... it seems to me altogether too bad to let the hard work and worries of past years go by the board, all on account of lack of care on the part of Avesta and, it seems to me, a shortsighted policy towards their customers.

The management at Avesta countered by pointing out the low turnover in the drilling steel stock in the United States, and compared this with the way the London company had been able to prime the South African market on a commission basis. Avesta's assessment of how the U.S. market worked and how the American customers reasoned was completely wrongheaded, Wilkens believed. In a later letter, he put it this way:

> What Avesta will have to do, before they will be able to get their proper share of the business available in this market, is to familiarize themselves with the American requirements and be careful in the execution of the orders they get ... the requirements on quality and appearance of steel are sharper and more strict here.

Something had to be done. Eric Sandström, a recruit from Ingersoll who had been in charge of the South African activities, was transferred to the New York office to develop the sales organization there. The stockpiling strategy was abandoned, and during the early 1930s, the company attempted to get rid of the stocks of stainless steel that it had previously amassed. The close drilling steel cooperation with CPT was ended, though CPT remained in the picture as a business partner during the 1930s. Sandström instead employed individual salesmen, each of whom would handle his own region. A high priority was to get away from the »CPT« brand name. From now on, »Avesta« would be the name to watch in the U.S. market as in the European.

The world economy plunged once again into profound depression in 1929. Many nations resorted to various forms of trade restrictions. The United States did the same. Import restrictions were severe in the steel market. According to President Roosevelt's industrial policy, federally supported investments should, as far as possible, be exploited to aid domestic suppliers. This throttled Avesta's prospects for sales in the United States. The status of licenses and patents surrounding stainless steel had became very unclear.

Sweden sealed a bilateral trade agreement with the United States in 1935 but this did not mean that Johnsons' steel business expanded. The issue of rights became a weapon in the struggle between Johnson and the other two dominating, and collaborating, manufacturers of stainless steel, Krupp and Firth Brearly. To be on the safe side and avoid further conflict, Avesta decided to let the New York company sell only pure chromium steel in the interim. Displeased with the poor results, Johnson complained in a cable. In reply, the New York office pointed out that it was not allowed to sell the quality of steel that was most suitable. In the chrome steel mar-

53

ket, the firm had a competitive weakness, since there was no stock and every order had to be shipped from Sweden with a major loss of time.

The patent rights that Harding had acquired for stainless steel ran out in 1936. Negotiations with ASS on exporting Avesta's stainless steel led nowhere. During the remainder of the 1930s, there was no improvement in Johnsons' steel business in the United States. When war broke out all trade was canceled. After the war, it would take many years before the steel business returned to normal.

When the steady income from steel licenses dried up in the mid-1930s, even more pressure was exerted to find business to fill the gap. Hedström, the number two man at the New York company, tried importing scythes, thumbtacks, toothpicks, clothespins and brushes. The trade agreements had lowered import duties on such goods. The market for plywood and other wood products was investigated. Hedström also looked into the prospects of importing a variety of manufactured products from Finland: horseshoe nails, files, bow-saw frames, circular saws, carving knives, chisels, oil burners, separators, mills, »as well as pliers, nippers and pincers.«

It would be an exaggeration to claim that the Consul General was enthusiastic about the business taking this tack; all things considered, he must have found such dealings alien to the Johnson tradition. The import of timber from British Guyana was a more welcome idea. This business proposal came from the London office. Since 1938, the New York company had acted as agents for Willems Timber and Trade Co., Ltd. Lumber from the Greenheart pine, which grew in South America, was considered especially suitable for shipbuilding. There were also gold deposits in British Guyana that interested the Consul General and gave the New York company plenty to do. Over the years, this interest would develop into the so-called Baramita deal, which ended up with a loss.

CHAPTER FOUR

Buying oil for Nynäs

Since its beginning, the Johnson firm had been in the energy business, trading with coal. After the First World War, it seemed obvious that in the long run, oil would be the dominant fuel. Johnson was eager to get a share of the growing Swedish market for oil products, petroleum, diesel and lubrication oils. The switch to diesel-powered vessels in the Nordstjernan fleet, which offered nearly twice the freight capacity of steamships, created a dependence on cheap oil. It was necessary to secure an oil supply at a reasonable and predictable cost. As the Consul General remarked in a January 1921 letter to Ekström, to be forced to renew an oil contract in a situation of high prices indicated a very unbusinesslike lack of foresight.

The procedure for supplying the Johnson fleet with oil involved having the ships that plied the West Coast of the United States carry oil to Sweden, where it was stored in tanks in Gothenburg. The oil could then be loaded aboard ships bound for South America, where refined oil was hard to come by. At the same time, the oil acted as ballast. Thus, if a ship took on a large cargo of, for example, coffee, the excess oil could be disposed of as the ship passed through the Panama Canal. An attempt had also been made to send special tankers from the American west coast to Göteborg, but this did not prove profitable.

In October 1919, Johnson had assigned Ekström to approach Texas Oil or some other independent oil company, preferably with shipping capacity, to suggest that A. Johnson & Co. become their agents for northern Europe. »Independent« in this context meant not allied with the various Rockefeller companies that had made up Standard Oil. Although legal proceedings before the First World War had dissolved the oil trust, the different companies created by the breakup were still looked on as a common group. The most important were Standard Oil of New Jersey (later Esso/Exxon), Standard Oil of New York (Socony), and Standard Oil of California (Socal). Foremost in the world market after the Rockefeller group were Anglo-Persian Oil (based on Persian oil), later to become British Petroleum, and Royal Dutch Shell, which had its most important oil wells in South America and the Indonesian archipelago. Arabian oil had not yet acquired any great significance, and Russian oil had not won back its influential position after the Bolshevik appropriation of the Nobel companies.

Standard Oil of New Jersey already had an agent in Sweden, and Anglo-Persian Oil had established its own agency. Ekström was ordered to investigate how to buy an oil tanker, how to erect tanks in important ports in Sweden, and how to get railway freight cars for distribution of oil to users. Negotiations with Texas Oil got under way, but progress was slow. Texas Oil already had a company in Denmark, and they did not seem to be enticed by any installations in Stockholm, Nynäshamn or Gothenburg. The Consul General grew impatient. He blamed the difficulties and delays – in a way so characteristic of him – on his staff in America:

> ... if we go in for oil, we should market both fuel and lubrication oil. The oil market is without question a lucrative one, and will become more and more so. We must have first-class representation for fuel, even though – in the beginning – we might have to

arrange it on a commission basis if the big companies do not presently see themselves able to lay out capital for installations in Sweden. In other words, I regret that no results could be reached … and that the deal is still in the same state. You remember that I pointed out during my visit to New York, that I like to see the completion of things achieve real results. It is most vexatious to watch negotiations proceed bit by bit, without any final goal being reached, because it means time and effort have been spent in vain, and we simply cannot remain where we are treading water in this fashion.

There were no principal agreements with Texas Oil nor with any other major company during the years that followed. The Johnson companies could avoid dependency on the big oil companies by integrating upstream, by having their own oil wells and refining oil on their own. In 1920–21, Johnson joined a Swedish oil consortium to drill for oil in Mexico. First the idea was to break the dominance of the international oil companies in Sweden. Soon more ambitious ideas took over. Oil should be lifted and sold to the great international companies, or drilling could be leased to them. But the costs for the exploration had been underestimated, and after only a year the venture was abandoned.

The failure did not diminish the Consul General's interest in Mexican oil. He was most interested in the possibilities offered by Magdalena Bay in Baja California, which lay en route from the Panama Canal to San Francisco. Rumor had it that production in the United States had reached its limits; thus it was even more important to get access to Mexican oil. Wilkens was ordered to go along on a Mexican trip for Scandinavian businessmen in 1924. He returned very sceptical about the establishment of operations in that country, and the plans for investment in Mexico were cancelled.

The Consul General's interest in the oil business was demonstrated in quite another context. The result was a substantial loss, maybe the price of experience. The lawyer Dudley Dupignac, in 1925 the president of A. Johnson & Co., Inc. (cf. Chapter 5), together with a French army captain named Cloquet, got Johnson interested in a project for selling oil on the European market. A company was started in the United States, Refiners' Export Corporation (REC), and in Europe a network of agents, linked in different ways to A. Johnson & Co's offices there, was to be set up for marketing. The managers of the offices in Antwerp, Paris and London – Jensen, Prudhomme and Samuelsson respectively – also took part in discussions of the project. Johnson was to have 20 percent of REC, while Dupignac and Cloquet were each to have 40 percent. A yearly profit of $100,000 was projected, and Johnson placed a credit of $70,000 at the company's disposal. It is, however, not quite clear whether the company was in fact incorporated.

The plans were rather nebulous, changing from one time to the next, and a meeting of the partners in Paris at the end of January 1926 did not serve to make them more concrete. No oil was bought and none was sold, but the credit was utilized by the extravagant partners in their marketing efforts. Johnson, always aware of costs, began to grow suspicious, and wrote to Dupignac demanding plans and estimates. Meanwhile, Jensen in Antwerp did some detective work and found out that Cloquet was not a »serious« businessman, which resulted in Cloquet's dismissal as managing director of REC. On closer scrutiny, the project did not seem to have the value Johnson had first attached to it. He now realized the importance of getting out of it immediately and taking a small loss, rather than losing big later on. Although Johnson had footed the costs of the project on his own, he suggested that the losses be divided according to the projected shareholding plan, 20-40-40 percent. With Cloquet out of the picture and his share distributed to the others, Johnson's part was 40 percent, and Dupignac's 60 percent. Dupignac, however, flatly refused to cover any loss, asserting that his role was that of counsel, not risk-taking entrepreneur. Johnson held his ground though, which resulted in Dupignac's renouncing the friendship and quitting his position as president of A. Johnson & Co., Inc. The Consul General absorbed the loss and reinstalled Wilkens as president.

Aside from the need to supply his fleet with oil, a new interest in asphalt strengthened Johnson's commitment to producing and trading in oil. Since the end of the 1800s, asphalt road surfacing had been tried in cities. Up to the 1920s, country roads were paved, as a rule, with gravel. However, as automobiles began taking over the roads from horse-drawn wagons, the Consul General was quick to see the opportunities this evolution offered. When a motor car tax was introduced in Sweden in 1922 and the job of maintaining roads became a public responsibility, permanent road surfacing began to seem the thing of the future. According to one estimate, SEK 650 million – in the 1920s equivalent to about $130 million – were expected to be invested in Sweden's roads during the coming 25 years, Johnson wrote to Wilkens in January 1926. There was big business around the corner.

Natural asphalt was found in Trinidad, among other places, and Johnsons would have to send someone to investigate the possibility of getting asphalt from there. Pyrogenous asphalt, on the other hand, was created from the viscous by-products that resulted from refining certain grades of oil. In December 1924, the London office wrote to the Consul General about the possibility of getting the agency for asphalt production in Scandinavia. Soon after, the question was laid before the New York company. Wilkens tried negotiat-

During the 1920s, permanent road surfacing, using asphalt, was quite correctly seen as a promising future business. Nya Asfalt was one of the Johnsons' companies in this sector.

ing with Standard Oil of New Jersey and Standard Oil of California, with no result. Johnson was also negotiating with a Canadian businessman for the rights to amiesite, a kind of asphalt cement, which could be advantageously developed from pyrogenous asphalt. In a January 1928 letter to Wilkens, the Consul General announced that he had secured those rights. Edvin Bergström, an American of Swedish descent, was employed as a consultant for the construction of a factory in Sweden. The New York company was now ordered to buy an asphalt mixer.

In Sweden, Johnson's oil venture was personified by Charles Almquist. The Consul General had made his acquaintance in 1927. Almqvist, who had fifteen years' experience in the U.S. oil business, had – on his own initiative – developed plans for building a refinery in Sweden. Now, in 1928, he was employed by Johnson, and under his leadership an oil refinery was speedily built in Nynäshamn. This was a major expansion of the Johnson Group in Sweden. It can be seen as an integration upstream with regard to the shipping line's needs. It can also be seen as an integration from the point of view of the construction industry, where Johnsons was already etablished on a small scale. Now new companies were acquired or incorporated, Nya Asfaltbolaget and Svenska Vägbolaget. Starting the refinery can also be seen as an entry into a new line of business, oil production and distribution, which in turn led to engagements in other branches of the transportation sector. The idea was to produce asphalt in the summer, while winter production would consist of lighter oils. Asphalt was a seasonal commodity, since road construction in Sweden was possible only during the summer months.

Now in possession of a refinery and with a growing fleet of ships equipped with diesel oil engines, Johnsons was in an even more fragile position due to the dominance of the world oil market by the large American companies. That stronghold was emphasized when

With his long experience in the United States, Charles Almquist, third
from the left, was the entrepreneur behind the Nynäs refinery.

the Standard group, together with Royal Dutch and a number of
independent companies, joined in an export cartel to stabilize the
price of crude oil on the world market. In response, Wilkens recommended that the Consul General buy a minor oil company called
Falcon Oil that had concessions in Venezuela. This upstream integration into oil drilling would secure access to crude oil at predictable prices. Oddly enough, the Consul General never reacted to the
proposal in spite of Wilkens' urging.

Securing access to oil might have seemed even more important to
Johnson, considering how asphalt manufacturing would progress.
In 1930, Wilkens negotiated with the Amiesite Corporation of

America for the license to market amiesite in Argentina, and the Consul General was seeking the license for marketing in Turkey, Rumania, Bulgaria and Egypt. Johnsons' newly established road construction company, Svenska Vägaktiebolaget, got a huge order for road surfacing in Rumania.

As an actor in the international oil market, the New York office had a potential role to play within the Johnson Group. But to get a standing purchasing assignment from Nynäs, it also had to compete with external companies, both in Sweden and in the United States. Asiatic and Standard of New Jersey had agents in Sweden: Svensk Engelska and Krooks. The important thing for Wilkens and his staff was, therefore, to find independent suppliers. The final purchase decisions were to be made by Charles Almqvist in Nynäshamn.

The oil deals that were negotiated from New York soon took their basic form. Beginning in August 1928, the New York firm of Harvey Carter was in the picture as an oil broker, having good connections in the market. The first shipment Carter arranged came from the Tidal Refining Co. in Oklahoma and got under way on board the *S/S British Earl* in autumn of 1928. Oil business involved a huge cash flow, which neither the New York company nor Nynäs could provide. A U.S. bank gave the necessary credits and paid the supplier, upon loading, against guarantees of three months' billing. That meant that within three months the oil had to be carried to the refinery, processed, brought to the market and paid for.

It has already been pointed out that, regarding the question of steel trading, there was little confidence to spare between the Consul General, Avesta and the New York company. Nor were the oil deals to proceed without considerable friction between the parties involved. The New York company was not to add any commission whatsoever to the prices quoted, a situation that for understandable reasons would create irritation in the future. Wilkens had to make a special request to take a commission on the freight prices in order to get the portion of the profits that his negotiations had won. The situation was the same that had once irritated Ekström: His company did not get the economic credit for his efforts, though from time to time it was judged by its presumed bottom line.

The other reason for mistrust between New York and Stockholm in Ekström' days was also repeated when the oil business got under way. At the end of February 1928, A. Johnson & Co in Stockholm asked New York to get hold of crude oil from Mexico or the Mexican Gulf. At the same time, however, they were negotiating on their own, an undertaking that in the eyes of the New York office was perceived as »bad and dangerous«.

In June 1929, Wilkens complained that the New York company had been prevented from placing a bid on an oil shipment, in spite of the fact that they had carried out prior negotiations without a hitch. By the end of 1930, Nynäs began buying oil through the London company, which the New York staff found out only by chance. They were irked by it: The price would have been lower if they had handled the deal. »It seems to me,« wrote Elis Gunnars, the New York company's second in command, to the ailing Wilkens, »that this transaction has all the earmarks of discrimination in favour of London.«

Thus began a triangular drama between the Stockholm company's oil department, the affiliate in London and the company in New York that would go on for some time. The feeling in New York was that Stockholm was giving them orders to carry out market inquiries, the results of which were later used as starting points for deals by the London office. In this way, Stockholm could put pressure on London, while at the same time offering them vital data on which to base their decisions. But this also meant that the New

65

The first delivery to the refinery at Nynäshamn, 7,000 tons of Seminole crude, was pumped ashore from the tanks of *S/S British Earl*, sailing from Port Arthur, Texas, in 1928.

York company was doing a great deal of work that it never got paid for. Besides, the company was losing its good name by working on deals that it was seldom able to finalize. The suppliers soon learned to keep their bids high when dealing with the New York company in order to preserve more leeway for negotiations with its affiliate in London. A long quote from Elis Gunnars, at the time assistant treasurer of the office, reflects the mood in New York:

> When I came back to town yesterday morning, Mr Carter called me up and told me that mr Williams of Simpson, Spence & Young had asked him for an offer on East Texas crude for Sweden. Mr Williams claimed that he could produce a firm bid of 55 cents. If Mr Carter's report is confirmed it means that the Stockholm office again are playing the same nasty trick on us as they did in connection with the Panuco business in January and the Venezuela business in March. In other words, we canvas the market for them, getting together confidential information and firm offers which we cable them. We are keeping them familiar with everything that happens and every fluctuation of the price. We are spending a lot of money on cables, we are writing them letters and we produce firm offers which we know to be the best that can be had. Stockholm transmits all this information to London and authorizes the London office to close at the figure we have mentioned as the best obtainable at the moment. I do not doubt that London will close these three cargoes and get the commission we should have had to cover our expenses and to reward our efforts. Plainly speaking, they are giving us a rotten deal, and I cannot help but feel that this puts the conversation we had the other day in a somewhat different light. In your opinion, I am under a moral obligation to the concern even to the extent where I have to jeopardize my chance to get back to Sweden. This latest inci-

dent, however, serves to again illustrate the fact that Stockholm does not feel that it is in any way morally obligated to us. Your sense of duty to the concern and my sense of duty to you has no counterpart on the side of the Stockholm office, and without support from the other side there is very little we can do here. I, for one, am not going to spend my best years working for this office under conditions like the present one.

The troubles continued. »The old trick« from Stockholm's side was cited in November 1934 as the reason why Carter abandoned his attempt to get hold of Panuco crude. At the same time, Hedström wrote to Wilkens telling how one Mr. Garfias had made a deal with the Johnson company, which subsequently, without any warning, broke the verbal agreement and sought other suppliers.

... He [Garfias] thought it was a very peculiar way to do business, which he told Johnsons in his letter. He said that during his fifteen years of experience he had sold about $50,000,000 worth of oil, and this was his first experience of this kind ... Mr Garfias admitted that they could not very well sue Johnsons ... but they would do everything to spoil Johnsons' reputation.

The story went on. In February 1935, a long dialogue took place between Stockholm and the New York company regarding a purchasing deal. On the American side, there was an increasing feeling that their reputation as serious oil traders was jeopardized by the fact that they seldom got Johnsons' consent to close any deals, not even on very favorable conditions. Bidding in New York was used merely for pressing prices, while deals were made in London.

During the last half of the 1930s, the New York company was used less and less for oil purchasing. In Stockholm and Nynäshamn, there were indeed plans to make Carter the main supplier, to expand the refinery, and to develop the European market, but these plans were never realized. In fact, little was achieved. In 1937, Hedström came to the conclusion that the oil the New York company offered Nynäs on occasion – often after a bid from Carter – probably was not suitable for the refinery, since no business had been done in a long time.

During the last years before the Second World War, Johnsons pursued discussions with Davis & Co., a company that had procured a good many delivery agreements for Nynäshamn, particularly for Mexican oil, from 1937 on. This contact led to plans for closer collaboration. Davis had a distribution network in Scandinavia – Skanditank and Suomen Petroli – that he offered to let the Consul General buy in exchange for a long-term, exclusive delivery agreement for Mexican oil. Davis also planned to build tankers at Swedish shipyards. Negotiations were conducted – to Wilkens' irritation – in part through the Swedish businessman Holger Graffman, managing director of AB Transfer, which was owned by Stockholms Enskilda Bank. No deal was forthcoming from these efforts, however; the war brought everything to a halt.

During the war, a number of international and domestic trade barriers were raised to block oil imports to Sweden. In 1939, a total of roughly 1,500 tons of oil was imported to Sweden, whereas by the following year, the volume had sunk to a third of that, 535 tons, and by 1941 only 131 tons of oil came in. The modest volume of oil imported during the war years consisted mainly of refined products; imports of crude oil stopped altogether. This, of course, damaged business for the refinery in Nynäshamn, as well as oil trade for the New York company. Wilkens' attempt to get permission from the American authorities to exchange a certain amount of refined oil for crude oil was not successful. Some business, however, was done in fuel oil and aviation fuel.

All trade, of course, fell off with the outbreak of war. All that was left were a few export deals to Sweden, which were carried out with increasing difficulty. Therefore, it was difficult to substitute anything else for the declining oil trade. After September 1939, the New York office examined the possibility of exporting American coal to Sweden, but the head office in Sweden determined that European supplies of coal were more suitable; importing coal from America would not pay. Certain import-export deals in metals – for example, import of copper sheeting and export of nickel – were successful. Aviation fuel and kerosene were sold to Finland through the Finnish-American Trading Corporation in New York.

Importing and exporting goods was not an easy business with the blockade in force. But ideas could be conveyed. In 1941, the New York company was assigned to seek exclusive rights (held at the time by the Refrigeration Corporation of Dayton, Ohio) to sell freon in Scandinavia. On New Year's Eve of the same year, the Consul General telegraphed New York, saying that he had bought a railway in Sweden and wanted blueprints of streamlined trains so he could begin building them. In 1943, he discussed getting hold of tobacco seeds to plant in Nynäshamn, and aired the prospects of treating carrots with hormones. In January 1944, the shipping company asked the New York office to look into getting the exclusive Scandinavian agency for Sikorsky helicopters and requested all sorts of technical information connected with running buses. In Sweden a bus company, Linjebuss, had been acquired by the Johnson Group.

The post-war planning for trade got under way in earnest during 1942. The important thing was to be prepared when peace came. New York reported to the Stockholm office about »quick-frozen foods«, something that might be an export article after the war. However, Stockholm judged that vegetables were the only foods that would be attractive to the European market, and as soon as production started up again in Europe, it would not be feasible to import them.

The U.S. company also approached suppliers to investigate the possibility of exporting chemicals to Sweden after the war was over. The chemical trade was important to A. Johnson & Co, in particular to the Malmö office, and the office in New York was reminded several times of the importance of securing supplies. After the war, it would also be necessary to import steel for shipbuilding at Lindholmen, a Johnson-owned shipyard in Gothenburg; later, the New York company was able to negotiate a competitive price.

Even before the war (partly in connection with the oil negotiations with Davis), Johnson had shown a keen interest in developing the Mexican market. During 1942 and 1943, the company worked hard to broaden relations with South America, particularly with an eye to increasing freight traffic when shipping returned to normal. In 1944, Johnson's plans to establish airline offices began to take form. It was thought that these offices would be able to provide the Scandinavian airlines with service while at the same time coordinating traffic with the Johnson Line.

As the war approached its end, it became important for Johnson to ensure deliveries to his refinery. In October 1944, the New York company was assigned to approach Petroleos Mexicanos and find out if they could offer crude oil for asphalt manufacture. In September 1944, the New York company signed an agreement with Standard Oil of New Jersey for the purchase of large quantities of crude oil of varying grades. The same parties later drew up a five-year delivery agreement. In the period immediately after the war, however, tonnage was scarce. An Allied official agency in London was responsible for alloting tanker capacity, and Swedish interests were given no priority.

CHAPTER FIVE

Communication, competence and confidence

As has been demonstrated in the previous chapters, a lot of difficulties met Leo Wilkens when he tried to pursue the Johnson business in the United States. It is difficult to judge the financial results that Wilkens achieved. Partly this is a consequence of the haphazard archival practices that then prevailed in the office. Various financial reports and budget proposals from the 1920s are scattered among the correspondence. Consecutive, continuous weekly or monthly reports are not available and may not have been written, to the annoyment of the Consul General. Compiled annual reports survive. It was, however, only in the mid-1930s that external accountants were called in. Price-Waterhouse served as the company's accountants from the 1940s on.

The fact that the picture is unclear is not, however, just because the weak source material. The opaqueness is probably part of, or at least an accepted consequence of, a conscious strategy. The Consul General did not want profits to be allocated to the U.S. company if it was possible to allocate them to Sweden. The choice was his: Much of the business in North America involved deals that included one or more of the Swedish companies. It was in Sweden that he needed the money, either – as during the first years of the 1920s – to save the different parts of his conglomerate caught in financial turmoil, or – as in the middle of the 1930s –to expand his interests and purchase new companies in a period of economic growth. Any profits, regardless of where in the Group they were generated, were, it seems, used to finance the strategy of the Swedish business.

Nevertheless, it seems likely that the New York business, in fact, ran at a loss, as is shown in Appendix 1, table 1. Wilkens never denied it when arguing with the Consul General; rather, he tried to point to different circumstances that might explain or excuse this state of affairs.

The steady losses gradually accumulated into considerable sums. The losses were treated as a debt to the parent company. Later, some of this debt was exchanged for shares. The share capital, which in the beginning was estimated at $100,000, increased in two stages to $370,000 by 1952.

Money poured out of the Group through New York. From time to time, this of course led to a strained relationship between the Consul General and his man in New York. It seems peculiar that the owner's patience was not worn down. There are two possible explanations, which do not exclude one another. First, one might suppose that thanks to the efforts of the New York office, profits were generated elsewhere in the Group. Then the losses in New York would be a question of bookkeeping which however caused problems. Wilkens was requested to produce both financial prognoses, which often were optimistic enough, and periodical financial reports, ending in a red bottom line. This lack of balance and the resulting image of failure year after year was no effective incentive for the president of the New York company and his team.

The second hypothetical explanation for the owner's endurance suggests that financial criteria were not the most important. Despite continous losses, the Johnson Group must have a presence in the United States to serve both as a potential resource for different

The Consul General on his 60th birthday, surrounded by his wife, his five children, and other members of his family on the doorstep of the manor in Avesta. From left: Mildred Ax:son Johnson, Carmen Ax:son Johnson (the wife of Torsten), the Consul General, Torsten Ax:son Johnson (the Consul General's brother), Bo Ax:son Johnson, Margaret Ax:son Johnson (the Consul General's wife), Axel Ax:son Johnson Jr., Margaret Ax:son Johnson, Helge Ax:son Johnson (the Consul General's brother) and Marie-Claire Ax:son Johnson.

market operations and as an information conduit. Having an office in Manhattan was simply becoming for a business group like Johnsons. It was a necessary cost for the supposed benefit of all the companies in the Group. This explanation indicates that the New York office should not be judged only as a profit center; rather, it performed the functions of an embassy. This, of course, did not prevent the Consul General from demanding from the company a profit performance that he doubted Wilkens was capable of achieving.

Confidence between Wilkens and the Consul General therefore stood on shaky ground. No doubt, to a certain extent both were to blame, but there were also problems of a more general nature and some generated elsewhere in the organization.

The New York office and its president had to play a role that was not very clearly defined. Wilkens represented the Johnson Group and its patriarch in a variety of industrial sectors of the vast American market. He was to buy and to sell, and somehow to gain or hire the expertise that was necessary. The strategy was quite unfocused, but the performance criteria were clear: Unless a profit could be shown, in principle every week, the office had not fulfilled its mission and was exposed to the Consul General's irritation or scorn. In the New York office, this resulted in a frenetic search for business opportunities even where neither experience nor competence were at hand.

As discussed in Chapter 3, the most important sales efforts concerned Avesta steel of different varieties and quality. Here the problems arose partly from the fact that Wilkens was not knowledgable enough about steel, partly from the difference in perspective between the production-oriented Consul General – Avesta being the apple of his eye – and the market-oriented New York office. Johnson simply refused to acknowledge the signals from the American market regarding quality, sales conditions or competition, that Wilkens tried to convey to him. Johnson firmly believed in his product and in the validity of his mainly European marketing experience. In a telegram to Wilkens, he phrased it in the following way:

... YOU SHOULD NOT ASK ME CONSULT AMERICAN BUSINESS PEOPLE THEY OFTEN CONSULT ME BESIDES THE WORST THING A

BUSINESSMAN CAN DO IS TO RELY ON OTHERS ONE MUST RELY
UPON ONES OWN JUDGEMENT AND NOT ASK EVERYBODY FOR
HIS OPINION IF YOU UTILIZE SUCH METHODS ALL BUSINESS IS
IMPOSSIBLE ...

The Consul General was stubborn and he did not want to acquire
– and during the financially harder times could not afford – the
more extensive market presence with representatives and warehouses that Wilkens demanded.

The most important buying activity for A. Johnson & Co., Inc.,
concerned oil. Being in New York, the company had a geographic
advantage. It was close to where most of the oil was produced during the interwar years, when the Arabian sources had not yet been
exploited. Here, in the shadow of the majors, the small, independent oil companies, with whom advantageous deals were possible,
could be found, providing you had the right connections. And that
kind of market competence was built up in the New York office to a
greater extent than in Stockholm. The problem was, as demonstrated in Chapter 4, that the office was supposed to develop market
relationships without having the mandate to close the deals. The
Consul General's quest for control and his unwillingness to decent-
ralize decisions forced the New York office to underperform and
prevented it from building market credibility. The tactics of letting
New York scan the market and London close the deals was, in that
respect, counterproductive.

All these sources of irritation can be interpreted as the result of
insufficient competence and poor communication processes. The
Consul General and Wilkens, the product and the market, the supply and the demand, were separated by a substantial geographic distance. Communication technology had begun to diminish the
effects of this separation, but during the interwar years, the exchange of information was still comparatively slow. Communica-

TELEGRAM

NR 177 FRÅN JOHNSONS = NLT WILKENS AVESTA NEWYORK =

AUTHORIZE YOU SETTLE AMIESITE ARGENTINE LUMPSUM 5.000 DOLLARS NO

ROYALTY OPTION BRAZIL ONE YEAR = AXEL JOHNSON = 20 W +++

TELEGRAM.
KUNGL. TELEGRAFVERKET.

STOCKHOLM 7 - OKT. 1930

newyork j68 41w 6/10 17 22 via göteborgradio

= nlt = axel johnson stkm =

amiesite have discussed with eriksson he recommends buying argentine 5000 without royalty stop brazil account weakness patents puricellis earlier work recommend not buying now but will secure one years option with argentine purchase shall i buy = wilkens ⊕

During the interwar years, the telegraph was the means for exchanging rapid orders and reports between the New York office and the Stockholm headquarters. The contents of the telegrams were normally repeated in letters that the Johnson Line captains collected or delivered when passing New York. Later, telephone and facsimile took over.

tion was built on letters, orders given in one direction, reports sent in the other. Often these letters were dispatched with the Johnson Line captains, who as a rule called in at the New York office when passing by. It took approximately a week to get a letter through. For shorter messages, the telegraph was used, primarily to confirm already known information or to convey standardized quantitative data, like prices or volumes. The telegraph was thus merely a supplementary device in a communication system requiring a considerable amount of mutual understanding at the outset. When understanding was lacking, the short messages exchanged merely added to the confusion.

The problem of competence grew out of the difference between production and market competence, the latter of which was only gradually becoming viewed as something specific and important in itself. Also, the situation illuminates the growing importance of specialization. It was necessary to have specific production competence in each segment of the market, for example, in steel or oil, to prevail against the competition. The amount of market knowledge also needed in the organization does not seem to have become evident to the Consul General, who relied on his European and Swedish experience.

These problems were not unique for the Johnson Group in the interwar years. A study, published in 1990, of Swedish direct investment in the United States during a later period, makes a comparison over time possible. Nearly all the findings from the later period are highly relevant to our case. Foreign investors in the United States have generally had difficulties in getting a good return on their investments in the short term, but they continue their efforts because they cannot afford not to be present in this technologically advanced market.

There have been distinctive barriers to entry, though. Domestic firms have often been bigger then the Swedish ones and able to take advantage of their scale. They have established brand names and networks that can provide necessary auxiliary services. The costs of building a sufficiently large distribution network have been considerable and foreign competitors have generally had to adapt their products to the U.S. market. This affects product prices, and in the U.S. market, the price seems to be a more important competitive weapon than elsewhere.

Swedish companies in the United States have generally been small, but have carried a broad range of products. The business objectives have often been described so vaguely by the parent company that the subsidiaries in America have had a fair amount of liberty of interpretation and action. This has provided a flexibility often appreciated by both parties, as long as the flow of information was efficient. But the differences in style and way of working between the two parties have often been so great that they have become a source of confusion and frustration. Thus, introduction to the U.S. market has never been a way to solve internal problems in the Swedish company, rather the contrary. Even large and internationally experienced Swedish multinationals seem to have underestimated the difficulties, the blame for them has often been thrown on the subsidiary company's management.

The circumstances – communication problems, differences in culture and perspective – that we have been discussing at some length, as well as the ordinary rigors of business life – that is, recessions, lost contracts, delayed deliveries and other mishaps – were often interpreted by the Consul General as evidence of poor management in the U.S. operation. It was a way of personifying problems that Johnson seems to have been prone to, which is typical of patriarchal management. But Wilkens must also be given his share of the blame for their frequently bad relations. His enthusiasm and patience often gave way easily. In 1924, in connection with the negotiation of a new contract, Wilkens wrote about how ill at ease he was in New York, and how he wished to move back to San Francisco. The financial results that the company showed too often strayed too far from the rather optimistic budget plans that the company drew up. Personification of responsibility was something that Wilkens was able to accept without hardship. He gladly saw himself as the Consul General's man, Johnson's trusted emissary to the great American market. In Wilkens' eyes, this gave him a status different from that of the managers in the Swedish companies. Thus, he found it hard to subordinate himself to the routines of the Group, much to Johnson's chagrin.

In 1925, the Consul General reminded Wilkens on several occasions that he must send in weekly reports. Wilkens, however, continued to send free-flowing letters whenever the urge took him. Johnson reminded him again about his instructions for how the reports were to be written:

> ... [I] desire that you, every Saturday, send me a report of the preceding week's work. I receive suchlike reports from my other offices, and also want to have them from New York. These reports should contain a list of the business conducted during the week, showing the profits of each sale, and the report should also state the office's expenses for the week, which sum should be subtracted from the profits, so that the true results can be seen ...

There is another theme running through this sometimes inflamed dialogue: the New York company's independence. From Wilkens' side, what was at stake was the right to work according to his own assessment of what the market required and what it permitted. From the Consul General's side, it was a question of his desire to run things, to control operations, as well as his demand that his managers show leadership ability. But, as Högberg notes in his biography on the Consul General, Johnson never wholly abandoned his skepticism about the business ideas that the men in New York presented to him.

As long as the New York company could not show a profit, the Consul General had a weighty argument – to use either for opening a discussion or for closing one. Without a profit margin, Wilkens could not win the freedom of action that might have released greater creativity in him. On the other hand, the Consul General obviously preferred to place profits in the Swedish companies at the expense of the New York company, whose business activities were expected to break even, not more.

The first major crisis in the relationship between Wilkens and the Consul General occurred in connection with Harvey Harding's activities. As was pointed out earlier, Harding had demanded to take over Wilkens' position as president of the New York company in conjunction with acquiring licenses for stainless steel. Things had grown tense between Harding and Wilkens. Harding refused to report to Wilkens on the pretext that he was on a personal assignment from the Consul General, while Wilkens became increasingly unable to assume responsibility for what was going on.

Initially in the face of this threat, Johnson stated his full confidence in Wilkens. At the end of March 1925, he met Harding and signed an agreement with him regarding his remuneration in connection with the Firth-Brearly contract. The question of the president's position was left open. Johnson assumed that Harding and Wilkens would have the issue out themselves. However, Wilkens demanded that Johnson speak his mind plainly, and was not at all prepared to step down: »I cannot see I deserve it ...«. He thought he could handle the expansive Harding as long as Harding did not obtain favors directly from the Consul General that Wilkens had refused him. Johnson was rather brusque and had no desire to interfere:

> ... You are responsible for Harding having introduced him and you have to arrange with him without mixing me up in this business. Please observe do not want any telegram from Harding or from you this respect and as manager A Johnson & Co, Inc, New York you must show yourself capable clear up this affair. I have had already sufficient annoyance this question. To me comes New York office and our affairs first, which have to be duly watched and brought in harbour, personal matters only in second place ... you have my full confidence ...

Nevertheless, Wilkens took up the entire controversy in a long and detailed letter, putting his position at disposal but arguing his case exhaustively. In the letter, he confronted the charges of incompetence which, according to the Consul General, had been leveled against him. Johnson's answer, still more curt than before, demanded that Wilkens and Harding come to an agreement, otherwise a third person would be appointed president of the New York company. The two combatants then proposed that the company be split into one company that handled steel, headed by Harding, and another that dealt in trading, with Wilkens as the president. Johnson rejected the idea and notified them that he was talking to »my man in New York« to find out if he would take over as president. He did not mean Wilkens. On May 4, Johnson let them know that »my old friend Dudley Dupignac« had agreed to become president of A. Johnson & Co., Inc. Wilkens accepted what he felt, under the circumstances, was the best solution, and offered to remain in the company as vice president and treasurer. On May 25, Wilkens stepped down in favor of Dupignac.

Back in 1910, Dudley Dupignac had acted as counsel in a suit that Avesta filed in the United States, at which time he seems to have gained the confidence of the Consul General. Thus, he now swept into the New York company as an expedient solution to a no-win situation, his only merit his long-standing acquaintance with Johnson. Dupignac spent relatively little of his working day at the company, instead devoting much of his time to his own legal practice. In the summer of 1925, he traveled in Europe. It was Wilkens who continued to oversee the daily work at the office and who was assigned to study the sales of steel under the tutelage of Walfrid Eriksson while the latter was in the United States.

The managerial problems in the New York company were not solved by Dupignac's appointment as president. Moreover, Dupignac was also difficult to work with. According to a long letter in his own defense that Wilkens wrote in March 1926 to explain why so little was happening on the steel sales front, several of the staff were ready to quit if they were obliged to work under Dupignac. It was not, however, those complaints that torpedoed Dupignac's relationship with Johnson, but quite different factors. Dupignac's stay as a kingpin in the Johnson company was destined to be short-lived, due to the REC affair (see Chapter 4). Wilkens was soon back as president.

Actually, Dupignac's »guest appearance« had little effect. Appointing him president in order to break the stalemate between Wilkens and Harding may have seemed logical enough at the time, but Dupignac actually did very little to help them function together. Instead, the problem was solved by the death of Harding. The operation that Dupignac introduced – oil trading – was not supposed to be handled by the New York company, but by the Europe-based REC. One might have thought that this operation would be taken up as part of the New York company's activities.

The idea was not new. At the beginning of the decade, Ekström had been assigned to investigate the possibilities of linking together independent oil companies in order to exploit the European market.

Wilkens' critical letters did have some effect on the Consul General's reevaluation of Dupignac. Also Philip Dean – the lawyer who had served Johnson for a long time in the United States, but who had been shunted aside in favor of Dupignac – helped open the Consul General's eyes at last. Dean, who was engaged by the company to settle with Dupignac, had known Dupignac for ten years or so, and gradually found him »unreasonable, unfair, greedy and unreliable in his statements«.

A new trust had to be built up between the Consul General and Wilkens. Complaints and accusations still hung heavy in the air. Wilkens felt he had to clear it once and for all. For a long time, he wrote to Johnson, he had had a feeling that the Consul General harbored dissatisfaction or displeasure with him as an individual. Wilkens now requested a straight answer, both with regard to himself personally and to the business strategy that he advocated. This time Johnson avoided the personal question and chose to point to the weakness in business routines in the New York office.

Thrusts and parries continued to be dealt out between the two. An exchange of telegrams concerning a potential deal in insulating paper for the London office could look like this:

Johnson: WHY DO YOU NOT SEND INQUIRIES FOR PAPER MAKERS FOR INSULATING PAPER ACCORDING INSTRUCTIONS FROM LONDON OFFICE THIS MATTER MUST BE PROPERLY ATTENDED TO TELEGRAPH FULLY AND SEND SOME TIME ENQUIRIES.

Wilkens: YOUR 11TH MATTER BEING ATTENDED TO PROPERLY AND INTELLIGENTLY STOP CONSUMERS HERE PURCHASE WHEN

AXEL JOHNSON INC.

IN NEED OF MATERIAL NOT WHEN SELLER ANXIOUS SELL STOP
HAVE SAMPLES WITH ALL IMPORTANT CONSUMERS AND IF
THESE AND PRICES SATISFACTORY WILL PROBABLY IN DUE TIME
BE ABLE SEND INQUIRIES.

Johnson: YOU NEED NOT SEND LONG AND UNBUSINESSLIKE
TELEGRAMS WHICH CAN BE EXPLAINED BY THREE WORDS FACT
REMAINS SINCE I TELEGRAPHED YOU 8TH OF NOVEMBER YOU
HAVE NOT HAD A SINGLE COMMUNICATION WITH LONDON OF-
FICE ON THIS SUBJECT YOU CONSIDER THAT AN INTELLIGENT
WAY OF ATTENDING TO BUSINESS TELEGRAPH IMMIDIATELY
WHETHER GRADE OFFERED IS IN DEMAND AND IF COMPETITIVE
PRICE.

On this occasion, the Consul General was in London and his telegram reflects the London office's faltering trust in New York. They
were not getting the help they needed, they complained – in this
case, to get in touch with a cable manufacturer in the United States.
Now the Consul General, using a still sharper tone, demanded to
be sent special reports from Wilkens:

Your weekly reports to me ought to be full of business, because it
is no delight to read literature in which nothing is found. There
must be a fundamental change this year, so that the office in New
York becomes worthy of the company and its traditions.

In a November 1930 letter to the Consul General, Wilkens stated
that he was having problems with his health. In February of the
following year, he wrote that he had tuberculosis, but hoped to be
back on his feet within the year. He was freed from serving as president, but de facto retained the responsibility for the company.
Complications arose, and in September 1931, Wilkens was operated
on. He was obliged to keep to his bed until February 1932. In May,

India House, in Hanover Square in Manhattan, was owned by W. R. Grace and housed the Johnson office between 1927 and 1935. Before that, the office had been at 135 Broadway (1917–20) and 17 Battery Place (1920–27).

he agreed to resign, but requested to be kept on as an advisor to the company at a small salary, which was a convenient arrangement in light of the immigration laws. Wilkens had been in the United States for 15 years, and could not imagine moving back to Sweden. He hoped, instead, to find work on the West Coast.

Wilkens' resignation never came about. He stayed on as president throughout the 1930s in spite of continued poor health. He spent the winters at a sanatorium in Saranac Lake, New York, and the summers at Black Pond, or at a family hotel in North Carolina. He kept daily contact with the Manhattan office through telephone, telegrams and letters. The assistant treasurer managed the company's business and wrote daily reports to Wilkens. Wilkens was still responsible for the company, and virtually all decisions had to be made by him. The lines between the company and his place of residence were kept warm. Naturally, this was not an ideal arrangement. Now and then, Johnson would look for a replacement. According to a memo of June 15, 1935, Fred Doelker, a W. R. Grace manager in San Francisco, was assigned to find a new president for the New York company. There is nothing to suggest that Doelker ever came up with any suggestion.

In 1937, the question arose again: Did the New York office have the »right« personnel? By the end of the year, when it became apparent that the company could not show a profit even in the midst of an economic boom, it was decided that something must be done. Johnson sought the problem in the organization. If they only had a truly qualified and technically competent person in New York, sales of drilling steel, for example, would not be in trouble. It probably would be best, Johnson argued, to send someone from Sweden to take full responsibility. Wilkens insisted that everyone at the company was working hard, but demand had dried up, recession was deepening and the stock market was showing signs of an impending crisis.

The Consul General was back on course again in August because of poor results and no profit gained. This time he decided to assign J. Kingsley Rooker, a member of the board of the London company, to prepare a change of leaders in New York. On being informed of this in nebulous terms by Rooker, Wilkens interpreted it as a knife in the back and counterattacked, armed with several other offers. In December, Johnson traveled to Florida, and then on to New York for the New Year, 1939. The sources say nothing more, except that 1939 saw »business as usual«. In all likelihood, the Consul General and Wilkens had the opportunity to talk things over in person, and Wilkens was given the mandate to go on. He returned to full-time engagement in the New York office in the early part of 1939.

During 1940, Johnson's interest focused on shipping and the threats posed by the Second World War. After the outbreak of war in Scandinavia on April 9, Johnson decided to set up a crisis organization outside Sweden to take care of the ships that could not maintain service to Sweden. Wilkens did not have the special competence that was required, and Olof Edström was sent to New York from Sweden. From Vancouver, where Johnson had bought an agency in 1937 (C. Gardner Johnson Inc.), the shipping expert R. Borchgrevink was transferred to New York. Finances in New York were attended to by Andreas (Anders) Högfelt, who joined the office in 1941.

The eldest son of the Consul General and one of the heirs to the firm, Axel Ax:son Johnson Jr., also became a member of the New York staff. Just before the war, he had stayed a good while in San Francisco at the W.R. Grace office, learning about shipping under the guidance of Fred Doelker. Although the intention had been for him to remain on the West Coast, he traveled to New York early in the summer of 1940 »trying to get office understand what I know you wish regarding the handling, upkeep, etc, of your ships«, as he wrote to his father. Preparations were made for him, by profession a mining engineer, to be given a Power of Attorney – to administer the shipping company's business in the United States – which he would later be able to delegate to some suitable person in the New York office.

In the autumn of 1941, Högfelt went over the books of the New York office and found several occasions for criticism; in particular, the real estate holdings in Black Pond turned out to be a bigger fiasco than Wilkens had let on. The value of the buildings had been grossly overestimated from the very beginning, and the lawyer, Philip Dean, seemed to have been legally disqualified from acting as an advisor, something he had neglected to point out. These questions developed into a deeper crisis of credibility. The Consul General furnished Högfelt with the authority to act as his personal representative, not only in questions of shipping, but in the New York office's affairs at large, »to reorganize wherever it is needed, and to take any measures … necessary, after having first submitted … suggestions to me.«

Högfelt found the situation in the New York office to be different from what he had imagined and very hard to cope with because of Wilkens' attitude. Johnson sent a telegram to Högfelt, which he was to show to Wilkens, explaining Högfelt's assignment. The telegram's wording is reproachful towards Wilkens for his unwillingness to cooperate. This upset Wilkens, who telegrammed back his version of the story. According to him, upon being asked, Högfelt had denied that he had been sent on any special assignment. Furthermore, he had avoided looking into the office's affairs, in spite of Wilkens' inviting him to do so.

In February 1942, the Consul General planned to reassign Wilkens to a less demanding post, for example, as an oil trader in Sweden. Undeniably Wilkens had good contacts in the market. After the war, the Consul General told his son in a telegram, that the position as president of the New York office would become so important that someone with more leadership ability would be needed to fill it. Högfelt, considering his general and international experience, was a likely choice. But nothing happened in the short run. Högfelt was sent to drum up contacts in South America, and in February 1944, the Consul General telegraphed Axel Ax:son Johnson Jr. to say that Högfelt should be made executive vice president and succeed Wilkens as soon as a suitable spot was found for the latter. However, over the long term, the company should look for an even more highly qualified president to run the New York office.

In June 1944, Wilkens was awarded the Swedish Royal Order of

After graduating as a mining engineer from the Royal Institute of Technology in Stockholm, Axel Ax:son Johnson Jr. was sent to the United States in 1937 to learn the shipping trade. At the outbreak of World War II, he remained in the United States as his father's emissary and representative. The New York office, which for five years had been located in the RKO building, 1270 Sixth Avenue, in 1940 moved to the Rockefeller Center International Building, 630 Fifth Avenue. The view through the window here is, for some reason, a photo montage.

Vasa on Johnson's recommendation. In his letter of thanks, Wilkens concluded with the wish that he would be able to continue to look after Johnson's interests in the United States. But the Consul General replied by requesting that Wilkens come back to Sweden – it had been seven years since he was there last – to discuss the New York office's future. In this context, and in rather flattering terms, Johnson offered Wilkens a position in Stockholm. Wilkens replied that he was prepared to go to Sweden and would begin making arrangements, but stressed that he did not wish to make up his mind about a suggested reassignment.

Wilkens began making a long story of it. He did not want to go to Sweden, since he was not sure that he would be able to return to the United States as long as the war went on. If he was not able to continue in Johnson's service, being stuck in Sweden would be fatal: All his experience was with the American market. He would be happy to discuss the New York office, both in terms of its past and its future, and he definitely advised against making Högfelt the president. This last comment made the Consul General formally order Wilkens to return home. Wilkens replied by offering to take three months' holiday, after which he would get back to the question. But he did not want to leave the United States. The Consul General agreed to give him two months' leave, but emphasized how extraordinary this refusal to obey orders was. If Wilkens did not agree to return to Sweden after the two months were up, his refusal would be taken as a resignation.

Wilkens' holiday took its time, and he did not return to the office until the end of November. By the end of the year, he still had not left for Sweden; according to him, he was having difficulty getting official permission to leave. By the summer of 1945, Wilkens finally did arrive in Sweden, but had obviously landed in the doghouse. He was not allowed to meet the Consul General. After spending ten weeks at Stockholm Grand Hotel without being granted an audience with his boss, Wilkens wrote a letter in which he thanked Johnson for the working opportunities he was being offered in Sweden. He said he understood that his mandate in New York had run out, but he declined the offer of another job, saying that:

During the years it has been my privilege to be employed by you, I have always striven, earnestly and sincerely, to conduct my work satisfactorily. It has, however, become increasingly clear to me, particularly during the last few years, that I have never the less somehow failed to please you and gain your full confidence. It is a very great disappointment to me personally to come to such a conclusion after more than twenty years in your service ...

It is possible that a discussion took place, but Wilkens stood by his decision to quit, and in November 1945 wrote to say that he had gone in as a partner in a company called Johanneson, Wales and Sparre. Johnson's intention was that Wilkens should stay on as an advisor on, among other things, oil matters, but nothing came of it. Wilkens left the company at the end of 1945 and was succeeded as president in New York by Andreas Högfelt.

Axel Ax:son Johnson Jr., Antonia and Toni on board the Queen Mary in 1951. During these years, the Consul General urged his son to return to Sweden, worrying that he and his young family were staying too long in the United States.

CHAPTER SIX

The new role

I<small>N REALITY</small>, Andreas Högfelt took over in New York in the summer of 1944, complying with the Consul General's wish that he concentrate on leading the New York office into the future. Wanting New York to become one of his most important offices, Johnson declared in a letter of August 1944 that it should be organized »so that it can usefully serve all interests of our concern ...«. At the beginning of 1946, Högfelt formally became president of the firm, but he did not stay long on that job. He had been sent to straighten out exceptional circumstances in wartime and had never had the intention of remaining in the United States. The same was true of Olof Edström, who was in charge of shipping matters.

During the years of World War II, Axel Ax:son Johnson Jr. remained in the United States. There he met and married Antonia do Amaral Souza, a Brazilian lady. In her he found not only a caring wife but also a wise advisor. In addition, Mrs. Johnson had very good connections in American society. Together they devoted their efforts to the New York company's affairs, frequently using their social life to make connections that would also benefit the business.

After the war Johnson Jr. stayed on for eight more years in America. All evidence shows that he loved his New York life and appreciated the relative freedom from the influence of the demanding partiarch that he enjoyed in the United States. He came to regard the American company as his favorite and was more inclined than his father to move the company toward greater independence.

In 1951, Axel Ax:son Johnson Jr. was appointed chairman of the Board of Directors of the New York company, but even before that he was the owner's direct representative on the spot. In fact, from 1948 on, he was himself one of the owners of the company. That he was not appointed president was due to diligence. For Swedish legal reasons, there had to be no doubt that the New York company formally was a firm of its own, not a branch of any Swedish corporation, although most business decisions were made in Stockholm.

For the first time, the New York company would have an American president, a circumstance that increased the company's prospects of operating according to American business logic instead of Swedish. It was a step on the way to more independence, a step that was doubtless easier for the Consul General to take when he knew that his son was in New York. Johnson Jr.'s presence could guarantee the preservation of Swedishness and the Johnson spirit in the company. A Swede was also named treasurer, a practice that would continue until 1980.

Axel Ax:son Johnson Jr. was very active in the search for a new head of A. Johnson & Co., Inc. Robert K. Kinzel was chosen from a number of other candidates. He was 43 years old and had a B.Sc. from Columbia University. Although he had some training in engineering, he had worked primarily in marketing, first for Union Carbide and later for Pan American Airways. He spoke Spanish and had many years of experience working in South America. Kinzel's list of accomplishments gives some indication of the direction in which the Johnsons intended to develop the New York business. The South American market was an enticement.

The closing years of the 1940s – with the New York company

under Kinzel's management and Johnson Jr.'s direct surveillance – was a period when the company recharged itself with energy. The groundwork for much of what would happen in the 1950s was laid during this period. However, Kinzel later turned out to be a disappointment for the owners and in August 1953 was asked to leave.

Robert M. Lynch was appointed executive vice president in the late summer of 1953 and president of the company in 1955. He was schooled in economics and had gained his experience at the International Freighting Corporation (IFC), a joint venture of Dupont and General Motors. Before he came to Johnsons, Lynch was working with an Italian brokerage house in New York. Having joined the Johnson company in 1948 as freight solicitor and ship broker, he remained the company's top executive until his retirement in 1981, and stayed on another eight years as a member of its board. Over the years, he developed a close working relationship and personal friendship with Axel Ax:son Johnson Jr.

New men were appearing on the board of the company, complementing the president, who was an ex-officio member. As mentioned, Johnson Jr. was appointed chairman in 1951. George J. Kraft and Vilhelm Björkman, who had followed Benckert and Colby in 1930, left the board in 1946 and 1949 respectively. In 1946, Charles S. Haight, a lawyer, joined the board and remained until 1968. Harald Björnander, the treasurer, came from Sweden in 1951 and stayed until 1966, when he was succeeded by Stig Sultan, another Swede. Walter S. Busch was a member of the board from 1955 to 1981. Ernest C. Arbuckle, dean of the Stanford Graduate School of Business and a personal friend of Axel A:son Johnson Jr., joined in 1963 and remained a member until his death in 1986. A number of persons joined in 1968, including John Walstrom (–1979), Paul Owens (–1974) and Norris Darrell Sr. The board was augmented as the business was expanded and its competence reflected the com-

Axel Ax:son Johnson met his destiny in the United States: Antonia do Amaral Souza, who not only became his wife but also an important partner with a wide network of social contacts in American society.

pany's strategy. The office staff grew from a handful of persons in the 1930s to between 20 and 30 people during the 1950s and '60s, subsidiaries not included.

»... to usefully serve all interests of our concern ....« The contents of this assignment in 1944 was certainly not the same as in the inter-war years. From the late 1920s on, the Johnson Group in Sweden had developed in several new directions. The established operations in trade and shipping, as well as in the iron, steel, and oil industries, now were augmented by activities of different kinds. As mentioned, in the late 1920s Johnsons had gone into the construction and building sector, partly as a consequence of the Consul General's interest in asphalt and road construction. In 1934, when the economic crisis was over, Johnson bought the Hedemora factories, which manufactured all sorts of machines, radiators and products of heavy steel plate. In 1938, Karlstads Mekaniska Verkstad (KMW), a mechanical engineering group of companies that produced various kinds of machinery but specialized in equipment for the paper and pulp industry, was purchased.

The Johnson Group developed greatly during the war. Among the more important new additions were the Lindholmen shipyards, the Motala mills (producing marine engines and other products), Linjebuss (a bus company), and IVK (the Institute for Plant Research and Cold Storage). Together with the older business commitments »Johnsons« now constituted a diversified group of industries. This widening of the Group's already far-reaching enterprises meant a great deal to operations at A. Johnson & Co., Inc. Now an even broader assortment of products and services was to be marketed. It was of immediate importance that the firm get hold of the competence that would be needed to represent all these product lines in the American market.

The New York office was used extensively as a general information source for the Swedish concern, as well as a pit stop for the Johnson Group's staff on their way west. It was taken for granted that anyone from any Swedish company within the Group could count on getting all manner of assistance and service from the New York office when visiting the United States. From time to time, irritation over this »travel bureau operation«, which seldom produced substantial gain for the company, bubbled to the surface. However, the headquarters in Sweden saw the New York office more as a mission, drawing great benefit from the all-round information about the Johnson Group's affairs that their »travel bureau operation« afforded them.

During his visit to the United States in the autumn of 1950, the Consul General summoned the staff to the legendary Waldorf Astoria Hotel in New York City and gave a speech about his vision of the U.S. company's future. A. Johnson & Co., Inc., said the Consul General, would develop into a strong, independent unit in the Johnson Group. Its fundamental business concept would be to provide the U.S. market with products and ideas that had been developed by other companies in the Group – the first KaMeWa propeller had just been delivered by KMW to a U.S. customer (see Chapter 8).

The speech had a major impact on Johnson's U.S. organization; in comparison to the 1944 statement, it marked the beginning of a new and more ambitious role for the company. In a subsequent report, Kinzel thanked the Consul General and stated that »many of the people during your visit had an opportunity of meeting you for the first time and have gained a new appreciation of the meaning and spirit of your concern.« In April 1951 Kinzel reported that he was working on the formulation of »an overall policy statement for A. Johnson & Co., Inc.«. No such document has, however, been found.

The Consul General's strategy was consistent with the one that his son had devised from his American viewpoint. In a letter to Lynch at the end of April 1953 – Kinzel was still president then – Johnson Jr. writes:

As you know, I wish the New York office, by and by, to become a full-fledged representative of the various components of the Johnson concern which do business with the United States. You no doubt realize that this cannot be accomplished over night, but

I am, here in Sweden, continually stressing the desirability of working through the New York office and in the case of Lindholmen I now call your company their agents. You will also understand that there are many older tradition-bound people in our organization here and that my work with many of them in that respect is up the hill.

The New York office would become more than a representative of the Swedish producers. Back in January 1941, Wilkens had suggested – having talked it over with Johnson Jr. – that the company actually begin manufacturing in the United States, on license, products from the Hedemora and KMW factories, as well as from external manufacturers. The market situation was ripe for such a move since many European manufacturers could no longer compete. Manufacturing on license would enhance the New York office's chances of turning a profit and supporting itself, and strengthen its capacity to run the agency for the Group's companies after the war. Johnsons did not seem ready to take this new step at the time, but it was to be one of the company's main lines of development during the decades after the war.

The idea that the New York company should become more independent had financial implications with a very special background. From the beginning, New York had never turned a profit; in any case, it had never been allowed to show a profit. Surplus assets were taken home to Sweden, except for the money that was invested in the stock portfolio in IIC (see p. 113). Changes in the tax and inheritance laws in Sweden and the harsher political climate at the end of '40s, made it more attractive for the Johnson family to amass a fortune in the United States, far from any socialist experiments.

Currency regulation was established in 1939 in Sweden as a step in the financial defense program. The idea was to be economical

Standard.
75408 NY.

In 1953, Axel Ax:son Johnson and his family left New York for Sweden. At the Farewell Party dinner table were seated, clockwise from Mr. Johnson: Julie Swiekard, Walter Busch, Florence Lemberg, H.G. Wangberg, Helen Desmond, William Gavigan, Charles Webb, Edward Novak, Loretta Kenney, Robert Lynch, Dorothy Beaton, Robert Kinzel, Lilian Canonica, Harald Björnander, Ester Cooper, Heinz Pantleon, Jan Lensselink, Howard Scott, two unidentified ladies, Ole Dormsjö and Erna Robinson.

with foreign currency, which was scarce. This restrictive monetary policy, which was handled by the currency office of the Swedish National Bank (*valutakontoret*), demanded that firms, in principle, take home any profits made abroad, and it was quite difficult to get permission to take money out of Sweden. The currency regulation continued long after the war was ended and became an important factor in »the Swedish model«, isolating the Swedish economy from the world market. The currency situation was aggravated during the summer of 1947, when there was a dollar shortage all over Europe, making the currency office utterly restrictive in granting permission to buy dollars. The dollar problem was to persist for several years.

Johnsons had continuously to negotiate with the currency office, just as other Swedish companies with business abroad had to do. For Johnsons it was important to remain as independent as possible in relation to the political authorities and to keep assets out of their reach so as to preserve liberty of action. As the Group was a diversified conglomerate, losses and gains could be balanced in these negotiations. For example, when the New York company on behalf of Nynäs obtained the right to pay Standard Oil in sterling instead of dollars, it greatly facilitated the company's negotiations with the currency office.

A good many of Johnsons' discussions with the currency office dealt with defining under just what circumstances the company could decline to take home profits that had been made abroad. The more independent the U.S. company seemed to be, the better arguments could be mobilized in these discussions. Also, a main task for the New York firm was to »make dollars« for the entire Group. To do this, it was not possible to continue just trading in the U.S. market. Business must also be developed between the United States and other markets, for example, in South America or Asia. But most important in order to »make dollars«, Axel Ax:son Johnson Jr. maintained in a letter of May 1947 referring to advice from both Peter Grace of W.R.Grace and a Mr. Reutschler of National City Bank, was starting industrial production in the United States.

Currency regulation was not the sole reason for the new position of the U.S. company within the Group. Amendments to the Swedish inheritance laws also motivated new arrangements. With heavier taxation of inherited assets, it was plain that it would be difficult for Axel Ax:son Johnson Jr. and his siblings to take over the Group intact. Therefore, on the advice of Norris Darrell, a corporation lawyer who later joined the board of the New York company, and following the precedent set by the Ford family, two foundations were established. The greater part of Nordstjernan's shares was put into a general foundation, which enjoyed tax exempt status thanks to the nature of its operations – giving support to research and other activities of public interest. However, the more important block of shares, those with greater voting strength, was put into a family foundation that was provided with careful rules governing representation and succession within the Johnson family. This structure was established at the end of the 1940s but was not in force until 1958, when the Consul General died. Certain companies, like A.Johnson & Co, were kept outside this framework and could be used in other ways or sold if necessary.

As early as 1948, the equity of A.Johnson & Co, with its affiliates (including A.Johnson & Co., Inc.), was shared between the Consul General and his sons, Axel Jr. and Bo. The father remained in control but became more and more dependent on his eldest son, Axel Jr., who was called back to Sweden in 1953. Gradually, at the side of the aging Consul General, his influence extended over the decisions of the entire Group. Also influential was a group of top executives. Most important for the decades to come were the financial director

Gunnar Westerberg, the executive vice president of Nordstjernan Allan Björklund, the Johnson Line head of operations Swen Lager-berg, and Per Norlin, an executive officer and board member of sev-eral companies in the Johnson Group. Together with the legal ad-visor Jochum Sjöwall, they formed the »inner circle« of the Group top management.

The Consul General died in August 1958. Axel Jr. became the head of the family and immediately dropped »Jr.« from his name. When the estate was distributed, the brothers became the sole own-ers of A. Johnson & Co. Axel was named president, combining this position with his role as president of Nordstjernan and chairman of the family foundations.

Because it had such grave consequences for the corporation, one more circumstance of a family nature must be dealt with here. In 1961, in conjunction with his divorce from his first wife, Bo Ax:son Johnson sold his share in A. Johnson & Co to Axel, thereby making Axel the sole owner of the firm as well as of the U.S. company. This gave Axel even more than before the inclination to regard the ex-pansion and capitalization of the New York company as a personal investment outside the family's influence. This may have increased his special interest in developing the American business according to its own logic.

CHAPTER SEVEN

Shipping

The outbreak of war in Europe in September 1939 had no immediate effect on the New York office's work, but trade was gradually falling off. The great change came in the spring of 1940, when the German war machine began to roll westward. Denmark and Norway were occupied, and the offensive was hurled against Holland, Belgium and France. By midsummer, the Germans controlled the European continent all the way to the Atlantic coast, and the Battle of Britain had begun.

Swedish seagoing trade was cut off by the German fleet's blockade. It was altogether too risky to venture a passage, and a long time would pass before negotiations with both belligerents resulted in a restricted amount of shipping (enabled by safe-conduct escorts) being restored. The blockade split the Johnson Line's fleet into two parts, one inside and one outside the line of demarcation. This circumstance allowed the New York office to play a new and important role, just as the blockade of the First World War had been the very reason for its establishment. Now, the situation called for the office to administer the Johnson Group's assets in the Western Hemisphere on its own.

The most important task was to keep the fleet running outside the blockade, preferably in waters where the risk of attack was not too great. The Consul General's instructions to the New York office, sent as a telegram in the beginning of May 1940, were as follows:

FOLLOWING SHIPS TO BE USED FURTHER IN FREE TRADE
BRAZIL COLUMBIA [SIC] CHILE EQUADOR MARGRET AXEL
ANNIE STOP IF CABLE COMMUNICATIONS WITH SWEDEN
BROKEN YOU MUST ARRANGE CHARTERING SAID SHIPS TO THE
BEST OF YOUR ABILITY IF POSSIBLE OUTSIDE DANGEROUS
ZONES STOP ALL FREIGHTS IN DOLLARS AND EARNINGS TO BE
PAID SPECIAL ACCOUNT NATIONAL CITY BANK IN YOUR NAME
STOP AMOUNTS TO BE WITHDRAWN FROM SAID ACCOUNT FOR
SHIPS EXPENSES AGAINST RECEIPTS SIGNED JOINTLY BY
WILKENS BORCHGREVINK AND NOTIFIED ME OR IF IMPOSSIBLE
MY SON AXEL STOP ...

In June 1940, the first year of the blockade, an agreement was reached in Moscow between the Johnson Line and the Soviet freight office, Sovfracht, to ship machines and machine parts from the American West Coast to Vladivostok. Some passengers could also be taken on board. Under normal circumstances, Johnsons would have used the firm W. R. Grace, its agents on the West Coast, but trouble with outward customs made it necessary for Wilkens personally to maintain contact with the U.S. authorities, located on the East Coast in Washington D.C. Thanks to the efforts of the New York office, *M.S. Ecuador* was chartered for a first voyage. The client was the Soviet trading agency, Amtorg Trading Corporation, in New York. During the course of 1940 and the beginning of 1941, a number of voyages were administered for the Soviet authorities. Return cargo, like sugar and fruit, was picked up in the Philippines.

After the German invasion of the Soviet Union around midsummer 1941, the risks involved in sailing to Vladivostok increased markedly. The shipping routes to Asia crossed waters that were under the Japanese navy's control, and Germany expected unequivocally that her Axis ally would close off this Soviet air vent. The New York company was urged by the company in Sweden – as well as by the Swedish authorities – to investigate alternative routes. However, with the Japanese bombing of Pearl Harbor in December 1941, any chance of maintaining this traffic in the Pacific was out of the question.

After the war was over, the New York office renewed contacts with Amtorg, Sovfracht and the Soviet Trading Commission on several occasions. The Soviets were interested in using the Johnson Line to serve their import-export needs. The New York office also acted on their behalf as shipbrokers for Scandinavian tonnage on routes that were not trafficked by the Johnson Line, which earned it a commission. In Johnsons' later dealings with the Soviet authorities, it turned out that the New York office's relations with Amtorg during the war were a source of good will for the whole Johnson Group.

During the summer of 1943, Olof Edström, at the request of Nordstjernan, began reporting information and technical data about tonnage that could be acquired as surplus material after the war. The American shipbuilding industry had been booming throughout the war to keep pace with the German submarines' pillage of the Allied transport fleet. The huge strategic operations during the war also demanded a vast tonnage capacity so that troops and materiel could be moved about. Obviously when peace came, a huge number of ships of different types, called C2, »liberty« or »victory« ships, would be offered on the market.

In February 1946, the U.S. congress annulled the restrictions on selling ships, and lists were made of all the ships that were for sale. Nordstjernan gave the New York office the task of procuring two liberty ships, preferably of Bethlehem Steel's manufacture, which

The *M/S Seattle*, completing a goodwill tour under the direction of Axel Ax:son Johnson Jr., reached New York in March 1949. Together with her sister ships in the so-called Seattle series, she was much admired for her unusual beauty and speed.

was considered good quality. The intention was to use these ships, designed exclusively for cargo, to haul coal to Sweden in order to comply with the Swedish authorities' orders that all Swedish shipping companies were to reserve part of their tonnage for fuel imports because fuel was so vital to the national economy. The majority of the ships that the Johnson Line used – i.e. combined passenger and cargo ships, built to ship general or special cargo and possibly equipped with refrigeration units – were simply not suitable for shipping coal. Carrying plain bulk freight was not something the Johnson Line normally did, but with a couple of liberty ships they would be able to fulfill the authorities' requirements. Besides, in the long run, the liberty ships might be used to traffic a sea route in the Far East. Högfelt had already visited the Philippines in the summer of 1941 to scout for potential partners. Another idea was to establish a route from South America to China and Indonesia serving refineries for vegetable oil in China, cotton exporters in South America, and so forth.

It was unclear exactly when the Federal Maritime Commission (MARCO) would allow speculators to inspect the liberty ships for sale; perhaps they would not be ready before September 1946. By deliberately not offering easy terms, MARCO was not encouraging any business that could be perceived as competitive to American interests. Johnson's advisers counseled him to buy diesel-driven ships, which – while they were not attractive to American shippers – corresponded to the Johnson Line's tradition. Högfelt and Edström were ordered to drop everything and leave for San Francisco to meet Chalmers Graham, the consulting engineer, and the W. R. Grace representative, Fred Doelker. Axel Ax:son Johnson Jr. and Björkman were also on their way there.

The Consul General found it hard to make a decision on this question. But, as Vilhelm Björkman argued, he would have to make up his mind. A liberty ship would pay for itself in two and a half years on a coal-and-coke route. A practical solution, Björkman thought, maybe inspired by Graham, would be to let the Panamanian companies, founded in 1940, own the ships, since MARCO would not let neutral nations buy any ships of better quality. The Panamanian companies could then charter them to the Johnson Line. Furthermore, the companies in Panama could accumulate profits from the business without having to pay taxes on them.

The companies in Panama had been founded for quite different purposes. The stock that Wilkens bought for the Consul General in the interwar years had been allocated to a firm called Industrial Investment Corporation (IIC). In 1941, for tax reasons, the firm's assets were transferred to a company, founded especially for the purpose, called Athos, in which Högfelt was Johnson's representative. In 1940 another Panamanian company had been registered, Vox, with Öhman, manager of the Paris office, Borchgrevinck and Wilkens on the board of directors. The purpose of Vox is unclear. Still another Panamanian company, Porthos, was founded towards the end of 1940 but remained a »sleeping« company. For some reason, however, the existing Panamanian companies were not put to use as owners of the liberty ships. Instead, a new company was established for the purpose in Panama, *Compania Naviera Republica, SA*, founded in February 1946 as an affiliate of the New York office. In June of the same year, *Compania Naviera de la Paloma* and *Compania Naviera Puerta del Sur* were also founded in response to the Consul General's wish that there be a separate company for each ship. The capital necessary for each new company, $10,000, was be taken from Athos assets, just as Björkman had recommended.

In January 1947, negotiations with MARCO had proceeded so far that representatives for the shipping line could inspect the ships. But some months would pass before the purchase of *Betelgeuse*,

In 1947, three liberty ships were purchased by Johnsons. *Alcyone*, shown here, became the *Star Alcyone*, which together with the *Star Betelguese*, the *Star Arcturus* and their followers became very profitable for Johnsons in the Far Eastern Service.

Alcyone and *Arcturus* became a fact. Money was borrowed from Bank of America by A. Johnson & Co., Inc., and lent to the Panamanian companies, a classic way of financing shipping. After being rebuilt at Lindholmen's shipyards, the ships were all given the first name »Star« and chartered by the Johnson Line.

In 1949, the ships were put into traffic between Japan and the Persian Gulf by a company called Far Eastern Service, owned jointly by Johnson and the Everett Line. The Far Eastern Service, which was a profitable business for quite a long time, can be seen as the first substantial business creation of Axel Ax:son Johnson Jr. But the deal was not without complications; in fact, it caused great problems for the Consul General because of the Swedish currency laws, which stipulated that Swedes investing abroad must get the National Bank's authorization to do so, and that profits must be brought back to Sweden and taxed there. In the eyes of the currency authorities, the establishment of subaffiliate companies was not expressly permitted. Thus, Johnson's dealings in this case were looked upon with great suspicion, a feeling that continued to characterize the relationship between the corporation and the currency office.

Successively replacing ships as necessary, Johnsons trafficked this route until 1978, when it found it could no longer compete profitably. In the line's early years, however, the New York office earned a steady commission from the Far Eastern Service, which provided a reliable income. Some of the profits went to the Johnson Line, while the rest were pumped into the Panamanian companies. Although they were formally owned by the New York office, the ships were considered the owner's private property. The assets, which were not taxed in Panama, were partly used in the Canadian investments made in the 1980s by the New York company. When the Far Eastern Service was discontinued, its ships were sold, and a tanker was bought and chartered by the New York office.

During the war, shipping activities had been the primary concern of the New York company. Besides acting as agents and brokering cargo for the Johnson Line and – in time – several other shipping lines, the New York company made shipping arrangements, at the request of its clients, for their cargoes. The availability of tonnage was very low, and the biggest problem in exporting from the United States right after the war was getting both export licenses, which were issued by the U.S. authorities, and transport licenses, issued by the Swedish. The question of which to get first developed into a chicken-and-egg riddle, not unlike the problems of exporting coal after World War I. It was not possible to get an export license without having a transport license and shipping arranged. On the other hand, a transport license was no guarantee that an export license would be granted.

In matters of shipping, the New York company worked in collaboration with the London company and the shipping line in Stockholm. Borchgrevink, who had supported the office with his shipping competence throughout the war, was succeeded in 1948 by the newly employed Robert M. Lynch, who, after a hitch as a trainee in the United States and Sweden, took over responsibility for shipping matters at the New York company. In 1951, Walter S. Busch joined him.

During the 1950s, the shipping market was concentrated to New York and London. In New York, where a number of companies were located downtown, some thirty or forty brokers would gather at the White Hall Club or the New York Produce Exchange to make deals. The telephone was important in this work. Often it would take twenty or more telephone calls to close a simple charter deal. In general, the market was very unstable. A strike here or some other problem there could quickly cause a surplus of cargo or cargo capacity somewhere else.

The program for the renovation of lower Manhattan, where the World Trade Center stands today, shattered the brokers' close camaraderie. Many of their customers moved to new premises uptown or even outside New York City – for example New Haven, Connecticut, and the brokers followed suit. With access to modern communications, business could be run just as effectively over great distances.

As shipping agents, the New York company represented the Johnson Line first and foremost. Since the mid-1930s, Johnsons had maintained an office in Rio de Janeiro, Agencia Maritima

San Francisco was Johnson's base on the North American west coast, where the shipping line was represented by the W. R. Grace office.

Johnson. In 1950, largely through Axel Ax:son Johnson Jr.'s initiative and Robert Lynch's good relations with his former employer, this office became the general agents for the IFC as well as for another North American shipping company, the P.A.B. Lines. A. Johnson & Co., Inc., got the job as associated agents for the two shipping companies, a commitment which was to last until 1957, when IFC was dissolved.

From 1950 on, several more commitments were made, all of which reflected the widening of the Johnson Line's sphere. Among them was the agency for Wica, the West Indies Central America service, which was run by Howard Aller. In 1965, the New York company was engaged in the Johnson Line's plans for a route that would link Scandinavia with the east coast of the United States, the Caribbean Islands and Venezuela, and would be trafficked by six Argentinean ships. New York worked through a subagent in Puerto

In the 1960s, Johnsons was a pioneer in container ships, a new technology for naval transport. Here *M/S Axel Johnson* near the Golden Gate Bridge in San Francisco.

Rico, and the route opened in July 1966 and was discontinued in 1971. In that year, the Johnson Line opened a route for shipping automobiles across the Atlantic, Car Carrier Service. In the Pacific, the Everett Star Line operated a route with the ships of the three Panama companies.

More important during 1971 were the negotiations that the Johnson Line opened with the British Blue Star Line and the Danish East India Company's East Asiatic Line. A year later, these talks resulted in the establishment of Johnson Scanstar. This joint venture implied a major reconstruction of the North Atlantic trade, in which the Johnson Line got the dominant position. Instrumental in the whole process was Cortland Linder, an experienced shipping expert recruited by Johnsons for that specific task.

Operations on the west coast of South America consisted mainly of handling cargoes for the U.S. copper industry, mostly for Anaconda. In the beginning of the '70s, both Anaconda and Kennicott reorganized the administration of cargoes to Chile, a change that hurt the New York company although it did not affect the Johnson Line. W. R. Grace (after 1957, the Grace Line) had long been the Johnson Line's agents. This agency was discontinued in 1969, when the Grace Line was sold. In San Francisco, the Axel Johnson Corporation, under the leadership of Cortland Linder, took over as agents for the Johnson Line.

For many years, the backbone of the shipbrokering operation was a number of long-term relationships with, among others, the Cziarnikow-Rionda Company, the Reynolds Metals Company, W. R. Grace and E. A. Godoy & Co. Up until 1973, the first three of these accounted for 80 percent of the operation. Later, oil shipments for Sprague played an important role. On the whole, the major part of the shipments came from South American ports, but the majority

To accomplish the Scanstar agreement, the New York office was ordered to find the »world's best shipping man«, and came up with Cortland Linder, right, who became the driving force in several of Johnson's shipping operations. Here accompanied by Robert Lynch and Göran Ennerfelt.

of profits were earned by the North American traffic.

The Cziarnikow-Rionda relation was the fruit of Johnson Jr.'s social contacts. He had gotten to know the brothers Arnold (Ronnie) and George Braga, who owned Cziarnikow-Rionda, Cuba's largest sugar producer in the pre-Castro years. The Bragas' business strategy was to produce unrefined sugar in Cuba or buy it on a speculative basis, for example in the Philippines, and sell it on the New

The tanker *Oceanus.*

York market. The Bragas proposed that Johnsons go in as shipping agents for Rionda. They wanted to set up a fixed route between Cuba and the United States and hoped that Nordstjernan would supply ships to traffic it. However, investigations revealed that there was no economic basis for a fixed route. It could be that Johnsons saw in the Braga connection a long-term possibility of getting work for the Lindholmen shipyards, but was unwilling, over the short term, to do more than charter ships for the sugar route. Johnsons did not want its assets tied up. After the Cuban revolution, the export of sugar from the island was cut off, although the Bragas' cargo needs remained. The brothers started buying sugar in the Philippines and refining it in the United States. The New York company had this shipping assignment as late as the 1970s, when Cziarni-kow-Rionda was sold to a Hawaiian company.

For Reynolds Metals, the second largest manufacturer of aluminum products in the United States after Alcoa, shipments primarily consisted of freighting bauxite from British Guyana and Jamaica, then shipping aluminum powder to Corpus Christi, Texas, and to plants in Washington State. Behind this contract was another personal contact, namely Lynch's acquaintance with Reynolds' marine manager, Don Woods. Reynolds owned a ship that the New York company chartered out and later helped to sell.

W. R. Grace chartered ships to carry fertilizer from South America to the United States, and cargoes for two bulk carriers that the Grace Line owned. Later Grace gave up shipping altogether, and freighters had to be found elsewhere to ship their goods. As for E. A. Godoy, before Castro took over, it refined and shipped iron ore from Cuba; after the revolution, this business came to a halt. Shipments of aluminum from Kaiser Aluminum to Europe, among other places, replaced the Cuban trade for the New York company, but from the beginning of the 1970s, oil transports would play an ever more important role. The company's own oil division, and later Sprague, began shipping crude oil and waste oil in earnest, and A. Johnson & Co., Inc., began handling Nynäs Petroleum's tanker, *Oceanus*.

The importance of the shipping trade – which during the early 1950s was the New York company's most thriving source of revenue – waned successively during the 1960s and '70s. Still, by the end of the 1970s, the New York company represented eleven shipping companies. But when the agency for the Johnson Line was sold in 1981 to a Nordstjernan affiliate, the New York company got out of the shipping business.

122

CHAPTER EIGHT

Naval technology

IF A SHIP HAS A STEAM ENGINE, it is quite easy to reverse the direction of the axis and thus change the function of the propeller. But if it has a diesel engine, that operation is much more difficult and will take too much time to be practical. At Karlstads Mekaniska Verkstad (KMW), purchased by Johnsons in 1938, engineers had developed a propeller with a controllable pitch in order to increase the maneuverability of diesel-engined ships which had become more common in Europe during the interwar years. During the Second World War, an initial drive was made to market this controllable pitch propeller, later known as the KaMeWa propeller, in the United States.

In January 1945, a draft contract was drawn up between KMW and de Laval Steam Turbine of New Jersey to manufacture the propeller on license. The idea was that de Laval would manufacture the whole propeller, not only the driving mechanism but the propeller blades as well. But this required a costly investment in addition to huge license fees, and since de Laval had been offered only a non-exclusive license, they were loath to enter the deal. A statement on the propeller's utility from the Department of Marine Engineering at Westinghouse seems to have been used in these discussions. Bethlehem Steel, one of the United States' largest manufacturers of propellers, also took part in the discussions, which, however,

Elov Engleson, at the center,
was the inventor of the KaMeWa
controllable pitch propeller.

dragged on and finally came to a standstill without any agreements reached.

Most ships in the American merchant fleet were still run on steamturbines using coal. They did not need controllable pitch propellers, so the market seemed quite limited. Nevertheless, in the late 1940s, when Johnsons realized that they needed to manufacture in the United States to get a foothold in that market and to make the coveted dollars, a renewed marketing effort was launched by KMW and A. Johnson & Co., Inc. This time they aroused an interest in engineering circles and among buyers for the U.S. Navy. In 1949, the inventor Elov Englesson spoke before the venerable American Society of Mechanical Engineers (ASME). In 1951, KMW was in touch with Farrel-Birmingham, who – together with the U.S. Navy – was considering giving them a trial order for minesweepers. A. Johnson & Co., Inc., also began advertising the propeller. The same year, the Warren Company of Philadelphia installed a KMW controllable pitch propeller on a rebuilt tugboat.

Now it seemed as if there might be a market in the United States for the propeller. Axel Ax:son Johnson Jr. decided to intensify the sales effort. A marine engineer, Howard Scott, was employed by the New York office to develop the business. By the mid-'50s, a special division was opened at the New York company to handle the sales of the KaMeWa product line. A campaign, launched throughout the United States, was combined with the search for a manufacturer who would produce on license. Bird & Sons in Massachusetts showed interest in the idea. This company was led by a Swede, Axel Andersson, who also owned an engineering firm, the Bird Machine Company, in South Walpole. In 1954, a manufacturing contract was signed with that firm, whose president, Fritz Becker, had already had dealings with KMW concerning equipment for the paper industry.

One of the first propellers built in South Walpole, Massachusetts.
In front, the production manager, Bernard Rivero.

The Bird Machine Company built two propellers, both of which
were delivered to the Lake Tankers Corporation. It was the second
installation in the United States. At Johnsons' New York office, the
KaMeWa department increased to include two engineers, and
marketing efforts were extended to Canada. The intention was that
any products sold in Canada would be manufactured in Sweden.
This strict market division, which later played a role in the relation-

Fritz Becker, right, was president of the Bird Machine company when it
was purchased by A. Johnson & Co., Inc., and was thus the first president
of a U.S. subsidiary firm. Here, celebrating his 75th birthday, is Becker
with Howard Scott, his successor, who joined the New York office in the
early 1950s as manager of the KaMeWa department and was appointed
president of Bird-Johnson in 1964.

ship between Bird-Johnson and KMW, had a special background.
A. Johnson & Co., Inc., was owned by Axel Ax:son Johnson Jr. together with his father and his brother Bo, while KMW was owned by
Nordstjernan and destined to be owned later by the family foundation, the income of which was to be used for public purposes. In
order to maintain the proper demarcation line between the different
companies, the notion of »arm's length« was used inside the Group.
Each affiliate company ought to behave according to normal business practices, regardless of whether they were doing business with

other companies in the Group or with external partners. Taking manufacturing business from KMW and allocating it to A. Johnson & Co.,Inc., or any of its affiliates, could be perceived as violating this strict principle, apart from the effect it might have on the results – and the incentive systems – of the different companies.

From 1954 to 1958, only a few propellers were manufactured, and the operation ran at a loss. All production was done by Bird Machine and forging and foundry subcontractors; Johnsons did not want to invest in fixed assets. In 1955, two propellers were sold to the U.S. Navy, and negotiations were begun with the New York, New Haven and Hartford Railroad for three propellers for tug-boats. In 1956, eight propellers were sold. A chief engineer and a sales engineer were taken on. A. Johnson & Co., Inc., began to investigate how to qualify for handling classified information, which would be required to compete for naval orders. It would also be necessary to manufacture the propellers domestically to get more substantial federal orders. The KaMeWa engineering department in the New York office moved to South Walpole and in 1957, negotiations started with the Bird Machine Company to establish a closer working relationship.

The next year, the manufacturing agreement was changed into a joint venture. On June 9th, the Bird-Johnson Company was founded with joint-stock capital of $300,000. A. Johnson & Co.,Inc., which owned 51 percent of the shares, appointed three of the company's five directors. Fritz Becker was named president of the new company, headquartered in South Walpole. Howard Scott, who had been manager of the KaMeWa Department, was made vice president.

Bird-Johnson ran at a loss, and soon after this shift in management, the owners of Bird Machine Company decided to bow out of the unprofitable alliance. In 1961, A. Johnson & Co., Inc., bought the rest of the shares for $75,000. According to the agreement, the new company would retain the old name, although it was now owned 100 percent by Johnsons. Fritz Becker remained president until his retirement in 1964, when he was succeeded by Howard Scott, who in 1979 was followed by Charles A. (Skip) Orem.

A license agreement good for ten years was signed with KMW in 1958. After ten years, it would be renewed automatically, provided neither partner asked to terminate it, which would require two years' advance notice. What Bird-Johnson paid for was the KaMe-Wa know-how. When the license was renewed in 1968, the fairness of the fee was questioned. Further, and important, development work had been done not in Karlstad, Sweden, but in Walpole, Massachussets. Axel Ax:son Johnson, however, insisted on the fee being paid and even rejected the proposal from KMW that Bird-Johnson buy the technology. The ties between the Swedish Johnson Group and the New York company were dear to him, but they were, as mentioned above, to be handled strictly according to the principle of »arm's length«.

In the early 1960s, a new product line was introduced at Bird-Johnson, bow thrusters, a small propeller in a transverse tunnel that increases a vessel's lateral maneuverability, thereby lessening its dependence on tugboats in harbors and narrow channels. Howard Scott had long argued the desirability of thrusters as a product line. The design was executed by Sven Åke Jardmo upon his return to Sweden following the hiring of Donald Ridley as Bird-Johnson's chief engineer. Ridley became manager of sales in 1964 and finally senior vice president.

In 1963, Bird-Johnson was still merely an engineering and sales company but the steady losses had finally become gains. A dozen or so people were employed, among them salesmen in Cleveland, covering the Great Lakes area, and in New York, and an agent in San

Bow thrusters increased the ability to maneuver ships, e.g., in harbors. A representative of General Motors, which dominated the tugboat market, renamed bow thrusters »tug busters«, which explains why from time to time Bird-Johnson's relations with GM were uncordial.

Francisco. A year later, employees numbered about twenty. Manufacturing was done through subcontractors after the agreement with Bird Machine ended. The management of A. Johnson & Co., Inc., continued to be strongly opposed to investing in fixed assets and shouldering employee responsibilities. This was their position even long after Bird-Johnson built its own plant in South Walpole in 1972. Up to 1979, personnel working in the assembly plant were subcontracted from a machine company in Walpole.

A new line of products – a third branch along with propellers and thrusters – was introduced when Bird-Johnson became agents for hydraulic motors. In 1972, the company was approached by Hägglunds AB of Sweden to serve as their U.S. marketing arm. The rationale of Hägglunds was that Bird-Johnson was familiar with the marine environment in the United States and the Hägglunds motor was a logical mechanism for use on oil rigs in the Gulf of Mexico. Bird-Johnson's motivation was to diversify their product offerings and reduce dependence on propellers. In 1980, after several years of increasing sales to the offshore industry, Hägglunds, now owned by ASEA – later the Swedish partner in ABB (ASEA Brown Boveri) – cancelled the licensing and marketing agreement and took over the U.S. marketing themselves.

In 1976, as a means of expanding its non-propeller business, Bird-Johnson purchased a rotary actuator product line and a leveling actuator designed for use on military tracked vehicles. After several years of unsuccessful marketing efforts, the rotary actuator line was sold. Bird-Johnson retained the military vehicle actuator, however, and in the late 1980s the U.S. Army began a major program to construct Armored Combat Earthmovers. This became a significant program for Bird-Johnson and the vehicle actuator has remained a small but profitable product line through the early 1990s.

Diversification is not what has characterized Bird-Johnson. The company was for all intents and purposes dependent on the defense sector's orders for propellers and thrusters. In 1964 a contract was closed to furnish propellers for six Coast Guard cutters. In the middle of the 1960s, the intensification of the Vietnam War called for a massive outfitting of the U.S. armed forces. In 1965, a series of landing ships (LSTs), represented the gateway to an increasingly close working relationship with the U.S. Defense Department. As responsible for purchasing propellers, the Swedish-born Naval officer John Strandell played a vital role but he was not perceived by the Bird-Johnson people as promoting the Swedish owned firm.

In 1967, three Navy programs were defined, one for maintenance ships (Fast Deployment Logistic Ships), one for helicopter carriers (Landing Helicopter Assault) and one for destroyers. Four different companies competed for the main contract. Ordering routines in the Navy were now amended in accord with the policy that U.S. Secretary of Defense Robert McNamara had brought with him from Ford Motor Company. The concept was known as »cradle-to-grave« contracting. For each series of ships ordered, the authorities also required plans for maintenance. Comprehensive estimates were required, but on the other hand, the winning competitor could count on a long-term contract.

Now it was imperative that Bird-Johnson's people find out all they could about the competitors while at the same time familiarizing themselves with the program organization that the Naval authorities had set up. The most important contract was the one for thirty destroyers, which would be equipped with gas turbine engines. For four years, the personnel at Bird-Johnson worked on a confidential basis with all the various competitors for the main contract. Finally, they were able to sign an agreement with the strongest of them, Litton Industries, to supply both propellers and thrusters for the destroyer program. An important contribution to this deal was made by Admiral Philip W. Snyder, who had left the Navy to work for W. R. Grace and was recruited by Johnson as the company's technical representative to convince the Naval authorities in Washington of the superiority of the controllable pitch propeller.

The 1971 contract for destroyers was followed the year after by a contract for an even greater number of frigates. But negotiations took a long time and required, besides continuous development work on several levels, a great many participants. Don Ridley's concluding description deserves to be quoted:

In summary, four years of effort using the FDLS as a learning vehicle and the LHA as a trial horse culminated in the prize of the DD 963 class CPP contract. From the inception of the effort in 1967, more than sixteen years would pass until the last of the thirty ships was at sea and the final contract payment received.

To get the Naval assignments, Bird-Johnson was required not just to manufacture in the United States and be eligible to handle classified information. It also had to restructure the leadership of its own organization. A foreign-owned company with aliens on its Board of Directors could not be considered for important Federal military orders. Thus, the board of Bird-Johnson was replaced in 1968 by »voting trustees«, who acted as the necessary filter between Bird-Johnson's operations and the Swedish-owned parent company, A. Johnson & Co., Inc. (Earlier a system of individual security clearances had been used.) The trustee form of organization meant that the Swedish owner waived direct control over the company, something that was – and in principle still is – foreign to the perspective of the Johnson companies' corporate culture. Therefore, the selection of trustees was critical. They had to be people with credibility in the eyes of both the owner and the customer. The authorities could, after all, reject anyone they deemed questionable. The first trustees were Admiral George W. Anderson, Ernest Arbuckle and Rodney N. Hatcher. In the Kennedy era, during the Cuban Missile Crisis, Anderson was Chief of Naval Operations. Later he was made ambassador to Portugal, and was now a national security advisor to the White House. He was contacted by Snyder, who had been his friend at the Naval Academy. Arbuckle does not need an introduction in this context; he left the New York company's Board of Directors to become a trustee of Bird-Johnson. Hatcher was retired from Citibank, where he had been in charge of business with Scan-

Charles (Skip) Orem led Bird-Johnson during the 1980s.

dinavia. Together, they provided the Board of Trustees with competence in three areas: the Navy, business and finance.

The desire to maintain competence in these three areas can be
seen in later configurations of Bird-Johnson's Board of Trustees.
Admiral Anderson left Bird-Johnson at the beginning of 1983 and
was succeeded by Admiral Alfred J. Whittle, who retired as Chief of
Naval Materiel, a post that is reckoned as number three in the U.S.
Navy. He died in 1993 and was succeded by Admiral Carlisle A. H.
Trost, former U.S. Navy Chief of Naval Operations.

Ernest Arbuckle resigned in May, 1973, to rejoin the board of A.
Johnson & Co., Inc. He was succeeded by Bernard J. O'Keefe, who
came from the engineering firm EGG, Edgerton, Germischhausen
and Greer. O'Keefe left in 1982 and was succeeded by G. Alan
Steuber, who was president of Prudential Capital, an investment
arm of Prudential Insurance.

Hatcher was succeeded in 1978 by Thomas F. Morrow, who had been in charge of international business at Chrysler Corporation, but stayed on only a short while due to poor health. Morrow was followed by Richard McGinnis, who had been chief of United Car, a member of the TRW conglomerate that produces auto parts. McGinnis was succeeded in 1990 by Richard I. Arthur, president of Sippican Corp., a company making electronic military equipment for submarines.

We can look upon the development of Bird-Johnson as a process of maturation, successive steps toward emancipation. Although Bird-Johnson began as a direct offshoot of the Swedish parent company, it gradually evolved according to its own logic. In the beginning of the 1950s, the New York company's operations revolved around marketing products produced by the Johnson companies in Sweden, but they also began to include producing in the United States in order to obtain the desirable dollars. Then a special division was established to sell the controllable propellers developed by KMW. When it became clear that the most important customer in the United States was the Federal Government, domestic manufacture was started in order to be considered for contracts. The relationship with the Bird-Machine Company was established on the basis of a license from KMW. In 1961, the American co-owners were bought out. At about the same time, the manufacture of bow thrusters began turning yearly losses into profits.

The next step in Bird-Johnson's emancipation was the effort to break into the military market, which made it necessary to isolate the company from its Swedish owners by means of voting trustees. The Swedish owners no longer had oversight of the company or its operations. The development of the propeller business was determined by the U.S. defense industry market. Since the 1970s, Bird-

Johnson has sold over 400 propeller systems for military use, supplying not only the U.S. Navy but also the navies of Australia, Taiwan, Korea, Spain, Denmark, Israel and New Zealand.

Breaking into the international market was not without difficulties for Bird-Johnson. The KaMeWa propeller was manufactured by Bird-Johnson on license from Karlstads Mekaniska Verkstad. While Bird-Johnson had the right to manufacture and market this product in the United States »and its territories and possessions«, KMW, represented by A. Johnson & Co HAB, was to do business with the rest of the world. In the early 1980s, the KaMeWa Sales Company was founded to market controllable pitch propellers worldwide. There were talks concerning a merger of KaMeWa, Bird-Johnson and A. Johnson & Co HAB, but they led nowhere. Instead conflicts arose.

In 1982, Bird-Johnson accepted an order from the Australian Navy for products that would be supplied by a subcontractor in Washington State. Perceiving this as a breach of contract, KMW retaliated by trying to get into the market for service ships for the U.S. offshore oil fields. In 1983, the Spanish Navy wanted U.S. Navy-type ships built in Spain. Because U.S. specifications of materiel were required, Bird-Johnson could fill the order, while KMW could not. In a similar fashion, there were differences over an order from the Taiwan Navy, whose ships were also to be built to American specifications. Again, it was easier for Bird-Johnson to get the order than for KMW. The Swedish company nevertheless claimed its right to the order and was supported by A. Johnson & Co HAB, which wanted the commission. No settlement between the affiliates was reached. The problems did not become easier when KaMeWa was sold first to Finnish interests in 1985, and later to Vickers Ltd, while A. Johnson & Co HAB retained the right to earn a commission on sales of the propellers. At the end of 1987, the agreement expired after having been in force for thirty years. The world market was open to Bird-Johnson.

Bird-Johnson was the only company in the corporation making a substantial profit during the first part of the 1980s. The task for the company was to use the unique competence it had to prime the naval market and to make money. The influx of orders led to investments, largely self-financed, beyond South Walpole. Bird-Johnson »integrated upstream« and – in 1986 – bought two companies that manufactured fixed propellers in foundries of their own. However, the company's prospects would change when the international situation was transformed towards the end of the decade.

CHAPTER NINE

Oil

PURCHASING CRUDE FOR NYNÄS had been one of the important legs of A. Johnson & Co., Inc., during the interwar years. The interest in this business did not diminish after World War II. On the contrary, demand for oil products increased rapidly all over the industrial world, due to the expansion of motoring and the switch from coal to oil for heating and industrial uses. This was a promising sector of the economy and Johnsons was prepared to participate. The oil business within the Johnson Group derived its logic primarily from the strategy of the Swedish operations. The oil deals done by A. Johnson & Co., Inc., were basically determined by the needs of the refinery that A. Johnson & Co had built in Nynäshamn, Sweden.

AB Nynäs Petroleum had been established in 1931 as a separate company, primarily to distribute gasoline and fuel oils – a complement to the Group's refining operation. New York cooperated with Nynäs in handling bunkering for the shipping line and pursuing chartering opportunities for tankers during the decades after World War II. New York continued to buy various grades of crude oil on behalf of Nynäs, thus developing a familiarity with the American and international oil markets that, the Americans claimed, was not as easily grasped from Nynäs' horizon. But all deals were normally made with A. Johnson & Co as middleman.

In the southern part of the archipelago, about 40 miles south of Stock-holm, lies Nynäshamn, a small industrial town that has grown up around the Johnson operations – i.e. the refinery, and the Axel Johnson Research Institute. As in Avesta, the Johnson family has put its stamp on the town.

The international oil market has generally been characterized by repeated and rapid fluctuations between shortage and glut. Political crises and shifts in power have played a key role; markets have sud-denly opened or shut. During the Mossadegh episode in 1953, Per-sian oil disappeared from the market. Three years later, because of the Suez crisis, Arabian oil had to be largely replaced by oil from other sources in order to fill the needs of the European market. The Middle East crisis in 1967 had a similar effect. For Nynäs and other refineries, such fluctuations could be troublesome but often the

New York company could get hold of oil at relatively good prices through its contacts with brokers and oil companies. All payments for oil from American companies went through the New York company, which received commissions on these deals. A kind of »tit-for-tat« trading also developed: New York bought oil from, among others, Standard Oil of New Jersey and Sinclair Oil, who in turn bought tankers built by Johnson's own shipyard, Lindholmen.

A. Johnson & Co., Inc., with its contacts in the technologically superior U.S. market, was also diligently used in other ways. In 1956, the refinery in Nynäshamn was destroyed by fire, and New York was asked to find a construction firm that could rebuild and modernize it. The refinery's operations were then focused primarily on producing asphalt and lubricants, as public investment in Sweden's infrastructure would vastly increase the demand for paving materials in the postwar decades. By the end of the 1950s, the New York company also began negotiating to purchase fuel oil and diesel (gasoil) directly for AB Nynäs Petroleum.

By degrees, relations grew closer with Royal Dutch Shell in Venezuela. John Walstrom, a Shell executive, was instrumental in this development as well as in the general buildup of Johnsons' know-how in the oil business. He later joined the board of the firm and remained a director until 1979. In 1962, a five-year contract was signed with Shell Venezuela to supply crude oil for asphalt manufacture. Nynäs filled Shell's asphalt requirements in Sweden. In 1965, a ten-year agreement was signed with the same company. For deals of shorter duration, the office maintained contacts with other oil companies.

Up to that point, the oil deals had been made largely through Harvey Carter's company, Oil Trading Associates. That firm, however, was dissolved in 1963. The relationship with Carter himself was maintained for some years. In the summer of 1967, following

Walstrom's recommendations, Paul E.Owens was hired and assigned to establish an oil department in the New York office. Owen's importance to the development of oil trading at A.Johnson & Co., Inc., can hardly be overestimated. He worked out a new program – together with the management of Nynäs – for supplying oil to the refinery after the 1967 war in the Middle East closed the Suez Canal. Nynäs was run on Middle East oil, but could hardly afford the transportation costs for shipping it in supertankers around Africa. A substitution was found in reconstituting Venezuelan crude into so-called »recon crude«.

The most important task in 1968 was to negotiate, with the acceptance of both Shell and Standard Oil of New Jersey, an »insider agreement« with the Venezuelan government. In 1969, A.Johnson & Co., Inc., was officially recognized as an inside trading company in that country, i. e. it had the right to buy and sell oil on the internal Venezuelan market though it did not operate drilling facilities or refineries there. Thus the company became less dependent on the big oil companies and the prices they set on the world market. A.Johnson & Co., Inc., paid a 50 percent tax to Venezuela on its profits from oil exports. The tax rate was, in fact, regressive – the more sold, the less the tax – and the company began selling crude oil to other customers besides Nynäs. The increase in sales created a cash flow that yielded considerable income in the form of interest. Even more important, taxes paid in Venezuela could be deducted against all income accrued by the Oil Division in the United States.

In 1970, the countries where crude oil was lifted began demanding a share in oil production profits. Soon this began to affect the business of the New York company. Venezuela, for example, raised taxes retroactively to 60 percent. Prices had to be renegotiated with all suppliers. The New York office then took on a new role in the international oil market. The strong fluctuations in supply and de-

Paul E. Owens was the man behind the Johnson oil business. Without him the company would never have made the profits of the 1970s that provided the basis for the expansion of the '80s. He died prematurely in 1974.

mand (and, consequently, in prices), as well as the increasing frequency of long-term contracts, often caused rather complicated bartering between buyers and sellers. Thanks to their expertise and personal contacts, the dealers in the New York office were able to help Nynäs out of difficult situations on several occasions and to earn a good deal of money for both companies at the same time. By the mid-1970s, business with Nynäs accounted for approximately one third of the profits taken in by the Oil Division in New York.

C. H. Sprague & Son Company, a venerable New England firm, had a history not unlike that of A. Johnson & Co. It was founded in 1870 to trade in West Virginia coal. In the 1880s, the firm integrated upstream by buying coal mines of its own, and later, ships were bought to carry the coal. As coal producers and distributors, Sprague was important to the American war effort in both World Wars. As late as 1967, the firm was the world's largest exporter of bituminous coal to many countries outside the Iron Curtain. Soon after, however, coal was phased out. All New England industries were converting to oil. Sprague's coal-mining properties were sold in 1968, and coal distribution ceased in 1970.

Sprague went into oil distribution in the late 1940s, engaging suppliers and building up a distribution network. By the mid-1950s, Sprague was one of the leading oil distributors in New England. In 1960, in Newington near Portsmouth, New Hampshire, Sprague bought ATC, the Atlantic Terminal Sales Corporation, which was later to become an important asset in the development of Sprague's business strategy. Through the purchase of other companies in Rhode Island, the operation grew even more.

From the start right up until the mid-1950s, Sprague had always been led by a member of the owning family. By the 1960s, a son-in-law had taken over and he divested. In 1970, the company was sold to Asiatic Petroleum, an affiliate of Royal Dutch Shell. This was considered a good arrangement by Sprague's management inasmuch as it secured oil supplies, which were always a source of concern to independent distributors. However, the purchase was reported to the Federal authorities, who – supported by the anti-trust laws – ordered Shell to divest its interests in the company. This strict ruling led Asiatic to offer Sprague outright on the market in 1971, whereupon the company was forced – literally – to open its books to any bona fide bidder.

One of the interested parties was A. Johnson & Co., Inc., put on the track by John Walstrom. Behind the New York company's interest was the opportunity to sell larger quantities of oil, thereby securing more advantageous agreements in Venezuela than were possible by buying only enough oil to fill Nynäs' needs. Besides, greater benefit could be derived from favorable tax deductions. Access to Sprague's distribution network would also increase A. Johnson & Co., Inc.'s flexibility in the market; barter deals were not uncommon, and Sprague could take charge of any grade of oil that Nynäs could not use. Earlier relations with Shell in Venezuela also colored the picture. A letter of intent for the purchase was written around Christmas, 1971. The condition, formulated by Axel Ax:son Johnson, was that financing would have to be done in the United States; no funds would be forthcoming from Sweden. Financing was secured through the Morgan Trust Company of New York. However, a personal guarantee from Axel Ax:son Johnson was required in addition to the customary committment from the owner's side not to weaken the financial position of the company. The purchase went into effect in April, 1972, and was paid for during the four years that followed.

Initially, Sprague's management had some misgivings about having a rather unknown, Swedish-owned company as their owner. Besides, the new owners could not contribute anything in the way of supply guarantees or distribution networks. However, it soon came to light that the New York company had a very important asset: know-how. Paul Owens and Arthur Hawk, his colleague and successor in charge of the Oil Division, knew the oil business. With the purchase of Sprague, A. Johnson & Co., Inc. gained control of a string of oil terminals in several ports along the New England coast. From these terminals, oil was sold to major industrial consumers and households, or to distributors, depending on the grade of oil and the state of the market.

For a long time then, conditions in the international oil market had been unstable. The producer countries were demanding an ever larger share of the profits from the international companies that owned the drilling concessions. The year 1973 was a dramatic turning point. The mobilization of OPEC (the Organization of Petroleum Exporting Countries had been founded in 1960, but had led a

Terminals are Sprague's most important fixed assets. Good locations along the coast of New England are scarce. The terminals can handle different grades of oil, as well as other bulk products like road salt, gypsum and asphalt.

rather silent life since), the dramatic rise in crude oil prices in conjunction with the Yom Kippur War in the Middle East, and the fall-off in production created panic in the market. In Europe and Japan – with their limited oil resources – the crisis led to new thinking on energy issues: Conservation came into sharp focus and alternative sources of energy were sought. For homes as well as industries, energy costs became an increasingly weighty budget item. But the oil companies made money.

During 1974, the OPEC countries got an ever tighter grasp on worldwide oil production. In many consumer countries, programs were initiated to meet the crisis by means of regulation and energy-saving measures. By 1975, this had resulted in an oil glut, and prices went down. In September, OPEC decided to act as a cartel and raise the price of crude. The price of refined oil products rose at the same rate, which caused problems for the producers. In the United States, consumer interest groups demanded new investigations to determine whether the integrated companies were breaking the anti-trust laws. By 1976, low consumer prices in combination with rising prices on the crude oil market meant diminishing profitability for large segments of the business. But in the fashion characteristic of the oil market, the pendulum once again swung the other way.

During 1977, high crude oil prices impelled production in a new field. Oil from the North Sea was introduced in earnest, and in the United States, oil began flowing from wells in Alaska. At the same time, the Saudi Arabian government decided to defy OPEC and increase production. Thus, 1978 began with oil in abundance, but ended in an anxiety that grew into panic during the year that followed. In 1979, prices rose drastically as a result of the ayatollahs' takeover in Iran and OPEC's decision to limit production. However, at the start of the 1980s, the picture had changed. OPEC 's power base was undermined, in part by its members' inability to hang together, in part by competition from new oil producers outside the organization. The '80s were characterized by relatively good oil supply and falling prices for crude. This was a boon to the industrial world and individual consumers alike, but not to the oil companies, whose profits returned to their normal level; and it was a source of regret for environmentalists the world over because the political dynamite of the energy issue was drowned in cheap oil.

The logic of oil trading was different from that of manufacturing. It involved greater sums of money and fostered a corporate culture very distinct from the one prevailing in the New York office and in the Johnson Group worldwide. The manufacturing contingent's attitude, as expressed in the phrase »that sloppy oil business«, was not without a touch of envy. The oil traders made money in the 1970s, big money, and they could afford the manners that went with it.

During the first few years of the 1970s, there was already an oil shortage in the American market. To fight inflation and help consumers, the Nixon Administration imposed price controls. Many major consumers – for example, local energy producers – shifted from coal to oil. By spring 1973, the oil shortage threatened to become a gasoline shortage, a politically risky situation in a country where driving a car was considered a constitutional right. In September, when the oil crisis hit the world, the U.S. Federal Government was forced to take political measures to protect the small producers. There was a risk that the larger oil companies, who pumped their own oil, would supply their own refineries and distributors first and foremost.

The Government revoked the quota system that had limited oil production, and then established a »voluntary« distribution system that would guarantee supplies to the independent refineries – the so-called »entitlements program«. It consisted of the following: To equalize crude oil costs between those with foreign and those with domestic oil suppliers, the former were granted »entitlements« which they could sell for hard cash to the latter, who were compelled to buy a number of entitlements that corresponded to their own production. The regulations were stiffened in 1974, and augmented by a special program designed to balance the small refineries against the big ones (»small refinery bias«, i.e., allotment of extra entitlements).

When the oil crisis hit, the New York company was well equipped to meet the challenge thanks to its position in Venezuela. The political measures also proved profitable for the company. In 1972, Sprague, having the tonnage and the terminal, built a refinery in Newington, New Hampshire. (The company also had refinery capacity in Wilmington, North Carolina, operated by ATC Petroleum. In ATC, Sprague was partner with some other companies, which were bought out in 1977.) The plant in Newington was actually a so-called »interface plant«, which connects different pipeline systems and takes care of any grades of surplus oil left in the system. Basically, it works like a simple refinery, a »topping plant« that separates regular crude oil into three grades.

Originally, Paul Owens – the oil expert – had planned to build an asphalt separator, and managed to convince a rather reluctant Axel Ax:son Johnson of the benefits this would provide. One argument was that a separating process could take advantage of the technology that Einar Palmason had developed at Parkson. The label »separator«, instead of refinery, may also have been instrumental in getting aproval from the local authorities. During the planning stages, however, it became clear that the asphalt market was dwindling, and when an opportunity to set up an interface plant presented itself, neither Owens nor the technical expert, Roy W. Waer, hesitated; after all, the equipment required was more or less the same.

The plants in Newington and Wilmington refined interface material and showed good profits. During the latter part of 1974, these plants were upgraded and classified by the federal authorities as refineries producing 14,000 barrels a day (slightly less in Wilmington). That made them eligible for the entitlements program, and gave Sprague the right to buy a certain amount of crude at a fixed mean price instead of the market price. Reapportionment to the benefit of the small refineries provided a federal subsidy of one dollar per barrel up to 10,000 barrels and a smaller sum for volumes in excess of that. On this, Sprague earned a good income. The program was discontinued in 1981.

In 1977, the U.S. Department of Energy was established with James Schlesinger – later to be Secretary of Defense – as its first head. After that, energy policies were a factor that influenced the prospects for the oil business in the United States, even though President Carter's wide-reaching oil program was rejected in 1978 and U.S. oil policy remained a question of regulating minor details. For some firms, regulation has been a boon in that it hinders new competitors from entering the market; for others it has restricted business opportunities. Sometimes Sprague has benefited from de-regulation, while in other cases, changes in legislation have had negative consequences. In 1981, when the subsidies to small refineries stopped (after Ronald Reagan became president), refinery operation was no longer profitable. The plants in Newington and Wilmington were shut down.

Another example of dependency on legislation is trucking. Earlier, it had been strictly regulated; anyone who wanted to start out as a trucker had to show that his operation was economically sound and that there was a demand for his services. Thus protected, Sprague found it profitable to distribute oil via private carriers, a fleet of some seventy vehicles at its largest. But when the Reagan Administration abolished these »barriers to entry« and anyone at all could go into trucking, Sprague was obliged to begin using common carriers.

The 1970s were very good years for the oil business at Sprague and A. Johnson & Co., Inc. The latter chartered its own tanker in 1976, adding two more the following year. By mid-decade, tonnage was in short supply and brought good prices. The ships were chartered with an option to buy, which the New York company exercized when cargo prices rose. Sprague bought two of the ships, while A. Johnson & Co HAB bought the third.

Until 1988, Sprague also owned retail companies, like Petro here, located in Providence, Rhode Island.

During the '70s, the New York company's oil interests were not channeled through Sprague alone. The better part of the frequently large oil profits were generated by oil trading, which was still handled by the office in New York. Thanks to the competence and flexibility that Paul Owens – and, after his premature death in 1974, his successor Art Hawk – developed, the New York office was able to make big money both for A. Johnson & Co., Inc., and, periodically, for Nynäs. The access to still greater refinery capacity, as well as to American distribution networks that the purchase of Sprague afforded, enhanced the prospects for succeeding in the world market. Oil that could not be used in Nynäs could be refined and sold on the U.S. market. All sorts of barter deals could be arranged.

Thus, the New York company could keep Nynäs supplied, even during the oil market's more turbulent periods, at acceptable prices. But in spite of this, the problem (seen from the American perspective) was that Nynäs and the Johnson company in Sweden did not always follow what was thought to be a correct businesslike approach, putting the U.S. firm at a disadvantage in almost the same manner as during the interwar years. (See Chapter 4.) The purchase of tankers, mentioned above, was one source of mistrust between the affiliate companies. From the American perspective, it looked like HAB had jumped in univited to take advantage of the tax write-off possibilities on one of the ships. From the Swedish perspective, it seemed obvious that the U.S. company could not exploit the tax advantages with more than two ships, and that, in any case, it would have been more advantageous for the owner to buy all three ships through the Swedish company. Other contributions to the uncertainty of relations were the frequent discussions in the early 1970s between the offices in Stockholm, London and New York and the representatives from Nynäs about how the Johnson Group's oil operations were to be run.

During the course of the 1970s, the oil business developed in many respects through partnership agreements, often supply agreements, by integrating backwards and by going into new branches of oil production. The refinery in Wilmington, N.C., was a joint project with Trans Ocean Petroleum, Inc., and the Ingram Corporation. In 1977, the New York company bought out its partners in the Wilmington plant. Trading was also expanded to Texas and California, but discontinued later when oil prices did not rise as expected.

Relations with the Venezuelan government gradually expanded, but were not wholly free from complications. In the oral tradition of the company, the story of Art Hawk's detention in Venezuela plays a prominent role. For economic planning purposes, the oil companies in Venezuela had to declare in advance how much oil they planned to lift during the year. When the market became weak in late 1974, the oil companies decided not to lift as much oil as they

After Paul Owen's death, Art Hawk became the leading oil man at A. Johnson & Co., Inc. His detention in Venezuela in 1975 belongs to the living mythology of the company.

had planned. The radical Venezuelan government saw the production plans as a commitment to deliver a certain sum of tax and deviations from these plans as a breach of faith. As a lesson to the others, without challenging the big companies, the government chose to bring A. Johnson & Co., Inc., to trial. Hawk, who visited Venezuela around Christmas 1974, was prevented from returning to the United States as long as the company did not pay the planned tax, although the corresponding export never occurred. He was detained for several weeks before the conflict was resolved. A. Johnson & Co., Inc., deposited the contested amount, $30 million, in a bank with the right to draw on the account as oil was, in fact, exported. In this way, the company did not lose much money, but gained good will with the Venezuelan government that proved to be useful in the long run. The contract was renegotiated in 1978. New York bought 20,000 barrels a day, which made it Venezuela's largest customer outside the multinational companies. A supplier agreement was also reached with Trinidad's national oil company for its low-metal oil.

The Oil Division of the New York company became a »fully integrated oil company« in 1978, when a number of oil wells were bought, drilled and exploited jointly with Saxon Oil. A subsidiary was established, the Axel Johnson Exploration and Production Corporation, based in Houston, Texas.

In 1977, management at the New York company began planning a plant that would recover and recycle waste oil. As far back as 1969, attempts had been made to exploit the evaporator, developed by Einar Palmason, for refining waste oil (see Chapter 10). A pilot oil recovery plant was set up that year in Ventura, California. In the California oilfields, water is pushed down the holes in order to get the oil up. The resulting emulsion has to be separated before further refining. Palmason managed to develop a fairly good process and effective equipment. In 1977, the idea emerged to use this technology for cleaning and recycling waste lubricant oil. The company EkoTek Lube was bought for that purpose in 1978 from Bonus International, and the Palmason process was installed. Factories were established in Oakland and San Carlos, California, as well as in Salt Lake City, Utah. However, by 1979, the project seemed to flounder; the process worked, but it was hard to get hold of enough waste oil. From an economic point of view, the project was a failure, and the San Carlos plant was shut down. Later, the company was sold back to its former owners.

Eko Tek turned out to be more than a business mistake, it became a disaster. The company was subjected to an FBI investigation, accused of – before it was acquired by Johnsons – having distributed recycled lube oil as if it were new and even of using other and larger companies' brand names. Substantial parts of the management staff had to be replaced. This was bad enough, but the alleged violations of environmental law turned out to be even worse. Before it became part of A. Johnson & Co., Inc., the company had simply dumped its polluted waste on the spot. When that was discovered many years later, all subsequent owners, including the New York company, were obliged to assume the costs, estimated at more than $50 million, for the cleanup.

The oil business generated and required a substantial cash flow. Profits were periodically considerable. Between 1968 and 1977, the Oil Division made some $70 million, of which $50 million was invested in other businesses. The year 1979 was exceptional for the Oil Division: Profits exceeded the projected budget tenfold, $82 million instead of $8 million. The better part of these earnings was brought in by trading ($63 million), but refining and retailing also earned far more than had been estimated. The Oil Division had secured supplies in good time and at relatively low prices, and reached transport agreements that were favorable. Integration upstream made it possible for the company to exert direct control over a certain amount of oil. Integration downstream permitted the distribution to end users of both light and heavy oils. According to Lynch's assessment in our day, the competitive advantage of the Oil Division was its high degree of flexibility due to its informal organization. It was possible to change plans at short notice and to take advantage of any possibility that appeared.

At the beginning of the 1980s, the oil market declined and the New York company, like most oil companies, lost in terms of volume and revenues. Difficulties were aggravated when the federal authorities accused the firm and several other companies of having broken the price-control laws. Huge fines were at stake, and negotiations dragged on. It was well into the 1980s before an agreement was reached. The risk of being brought to trial incurred extra expense; every business transaction made had to be documented in detail.

Star Capella, one of Sprague's own tankers.

Thus in the '80s, the New York company's oil business was on the decline. It was necessary to shrink the operation. The tankers were sold, the refineries were shut down, oil production was decreased and economized. The sale of Sprague was considered, but on the other hand, it looked as though restructured energy operations – sometimes combined with hydroelectric or thermal power stations – might provide relatively good earnings over the long term. Besides, oil prices could rise again; the world oil market showed no sign of impending stability in the early '80s.

In 1982, A. Johnson & Co HAB – with the help of New York – opened an office in London for international oil trading. This joint venture was a compromise, and turned out – as compromises often do – to be a failure. The New York company would have preferred to develop its U.S. interests instead of joining forces with HAB in

Henry M. Powers, president of Sprague until 1986.

the international market. The management of HAB was more inclined to see the synergies in close cooperation because of the
Group's oil operation in Sweden and its relations with the Soviet
Union and other European suppliers. The joint venture was finally
sold to Axel Johnson AB in 1988. Oil trading in the New York office
was continued through the Axel Johnson Energy Corporation, a
new subsidiary led by Geoffry T. Magrath, who had joined A. Johnson & Co., Inc., as treasurer in 1980.

In 1980, after a ten year hiatus, industrial coal returned to New
England. Large New England paper mills and cement plants would
begin converting to coal as a cheaper fuel. Sprague was well positioned with its terminals and business expertise to participate in this
market. The company, since 1979 at new premises in Portsmouth,
New Hampshire, brought the first shipload of waterborne coal to
its Searsport, Maine, terminal.

Sprague also continued handling, storing and transshipping both solid and liquid bulk cargos such as gypsum, road salt or liquids for use in the paper industry. The terminals were Sprague's key assets and could be adapted to handling a wide variety of bulk commodities depending on demand. By 1989, oil trading had given way to a more customer-based distribution business. The plan of operation was revamped to selling light and heavy oil and waterborne coal, and maximizing utilization of the company's terminals by providing materials-handling services to New England's industries.

CHAPTER TEN

Environmental technology

THE PURCHASE of Parkson Corporation cannot easily be explained from the perspective of either a Swedish or an American industrial strategy within the framework of the Johnson Group. The connection to the development work being done at the Axel Johnson Institute for Industrial Research in Nynäshamn was more likely a result of the purchase than the reason for it. According to Lynch, the motive for buying Parkson lay in England. There, the Axel Johnson Company Ltd. produced equipment for the dairy industry. In the immediate neighborhood of the factory was a plant owned and run by Parkson's English affiliate, a plant that Johnsons was avid to get hold of for the expansion of its English business. One way to do this was by buying the parent company, Parkson, from its owners, Parker Pen Company, in Wisconsin. Other sources point to the standing orders for Lynch to look for good business opportunities, the proximity to the house that the New York company had bought for Axel Ax:son Johnson in Naples, Florida, and the good personal understanding that had developed between Lynch and the entrepreneur at Parkson, Einar Palmason. Be that as it may, in 1967 the New York company got a Floridian problem child on its hands, which bloomed into a profitable and stable operation only after twelve years of patience.

Palmason Industrial Equipment Company (PIECO) was started

Einar Palmason, right, and Carl Evert Gustafsson started Parkson.

in 1958 in Fort Lauderdale, Florida, by Einar Henry Palmason, a Canadian of Icelandic descent. Palmason was a chemical engineer and an inventor with experience at the British company Unilever. PIECO's mission was to develop and market one of his products, the evaporator, a piece of equipment for removing liquid from solutions that could not be subjected to prolonged heating. The solution was let in between a number of hollow parallel plates, rapidly heated with steam, and the water evaporated. The device's uses included, for example, concentration of fruit juices and separation of water from oil. The energy costs were, however, rather high, and the fruit juice application was never economical. The most frequent use turned out to be the concentration of latex used in the fabrication of paints.

PIECO became a division of the American Heat Reclaiming Company, which sold the company to the Parker Pen Company of Wisconsin in June 1962. Palmason remained in the management of the firm, the name of which was changed to Parkson Industrial Equipment Co. Parker Pen installed a professional organization around the inventor and introduced strategic plans for sales, personnel management and research, with the objective of finding uses for the evaporator in industries other than food processing. An English company, the Daniels Group, was approached about a joint project: manufacturing and marketing the evaporator in Europe. Thus, the already mentioned firm, Daniels Parkson Ltd, was founded in Dartford, Kent, not far from the Axel Johnson Co., Ltd., factory.

Parkson's production was a mite out of character for Parker Pen. During 1965, Parker negotiated with Lavalco and other manufacturers for the sale of Parkson, but in vain. In February 1967, A. Johnson & Co., Inc., purchased the company for $734,000 – the share capital was $100,000 – and bought the Daniels Group out of the English joint venture. In May, Axel Ax:son Johnson took over as chairman of the board, and installed as directors Robert M. Lynch, Ernest C. Arbuckle, Einar Palmason and Börje Wahlström. Palmason retained his post as president, and Stig Sultan was made secretary-treasurer. In 1969, the company – which was reregistered from Florida to Delaware – was named the Parkson Corporation.

The consensus of the board was that Parkson lacked competent personnel in key positions and new recruitment was absolutely necessary. A managing director was needed, certainly; Palmason seemed to be the archetype of the financially benighted inventor, though he was also a good salesman. His estimate that the company would go from losing money to breaking even as soon as 1967 was entirely too optimistic. Even during the next few years, Parkson's management was not able to turn the red bottom line into black. Palmason was losing credibility. In April 1969, he was succeeded by Carl Evert Gustafsson as president, and instead became a director of the board. As president of the Axel Johnson Co., Ltd., London, Gustafson, a Swedish metallurgical engineer, had been instrumental in the acquisition of Parkson and thus had a moral responsibility to show that the idea was good. The chemical engineer, George Gebauer, became vice president in charge of »new business«.

However, Parkson continued to operate at a loss for a long time.

Each year, money from the New York company had to be pumped into the ailing subsidiary. Sales of the evaporator were nothing like what Palmason had promised. There were some ideas of taking on new product lines, like hamburger and frying machines, but they failed due to lack of market know-how. At an emergency meeting held in August 1970, Axel Ax:son Johnson declared his view of the problem in a way that was as typical for him as it had been for his father, the Consul General. Personal characteristics were given great weight in the definition of problems:

> Mr. Johnson questioned in some depth how the company goes about marketing its products and who holds the responsibility for sales. He questioned whether the company was going about marketing in the right way and he also questioned whether the sales manager was a strong man. He pointed out that not only did a company need a good product, but in his opinion, it must have and maintain good friends in industry ...

As yet, no radical changes had been implemented in the organization, but all efforts would now be mobilized to strengthen the market performance. A younger marketing manager was to be employed at once, and if the situation did not improve within the following year, a more experienced advisor would also be hired on.

The solution to the problems was, however, not to be found in marketing but, to the contrary, in R&D and innovation in production. The light would come from Sweden, from the Axel Johnson Institute for Industrial Research (AJI) in Nynäshamn. This institute was set up in 1963 primarily to develop plans for nuclear energy, but it was also working on a wider range of research that could be useful to the Johnson Group of companies. It was owned by the shipping company, Nordstjernan, but worldwide marketing of its technology was handled through A. Johnson & Co HAB in Stockholm. It turned out to be, in a way, the central R&D resource within the Johnson Group, and it brought to the U.S. company, among other products, the separators and the tungsten project (more of which in Chapter 11).

It was natural that in order to improve the evaporator, the management of Parkson contacted the institute. There the Parkson representatives, among them Dave Ruths, became interested in some of the Institute's technologies, especially the separators, including the Lamella Gravity Settler. In the autumn of 1969, there is a general understanding recorded between the Institute and the New York company specifying that Parkson would market the Institute's products in the United States, Canada and Mexico. At Parkson an AJI division was established with a staff of three men and the mission of placing the Institute's licenses with U.S. manufacturers. The staff's plan was to acquire some of the licenses for Parkson, especially the Lamella, though that may not have been the intention in Nynäshamn.

During the summer of 1970, formal negotiations were opened with the Institute. At first its president, nuclear engineer Olof Hörmander, was not at all disposed to let the Lamella licenses go to a small, rather unknown company in Florida. Hörmander ran the institute in compliance with the Johnsons' specific demands for short-term profitability and an arm's-length's relationship, and the fact that Parkson was – as it were – »a member of the family« left him unimpressed. Until the summer of 1971, Parkson worked on finding other licensees. Then a new attempt was made to secure the Lamella licenses for Parkson, and Hörmander and his staff, Gunnar Ågård, Lars Ramquist and Bo Forsell, went along with the idea. A letter of intent was signed, followed by an agreement later in the autumn. The agreement was reached in a thoroughly businesslike fashion. Parkson got the licenses by making the highest bid. The

The Lamella was the
first profitable product
manufactured and dis-
tributed by Parkson.

price was $200,000 for each of the two Lamella products, to be
paid over 5 years; the down payment was $100,000. The Institute
would be getting rather good royalties, and A. Johnson & Co HAB
would get a commission on any licenses sold. Parkson had the right
to terminate the agreement after 18 months.

Lamella technology dealt with a new approach to an old tech-
nique – removing unwanted solids from water by simple gravity
settling. Conventional settling required large, cumbersome field-
constructed tanks because the liquid had to be held for four to eight
hours for the settling process to be completed. The Lamella con-

cept compressed the settling volume into 5 to 10 percent of the space normally required, often allowing the use of much less expensive, factory-assembled equipment.

The Lamella line became the basis for Parkson's continued existence. A special organization was set up for the new products. The market in the United States was divided. Most important was the private sector – i.e., industrial companies, mainly in the chemical, metals finishing and steel businesses, that treated their own waste stream. The other sector was municipalities – i.e., locally owned drinking water and sewage treatment plants. Difficulties arose in adapting the technology due to the different states' legislation. Marketing depended on having agents all around the country doing demonstrations, documenting the technology, attending fairs and exhibitions, advertising in the trade papers, printing brochures, and trying to obtain media coverage for the new products.

But Parkson was still costing the New York company money without turning a profit. The strategy was tightened. At a meeting of the Board of Directors in May 1973, it was decided that Parkson would, in the future, devote its efforts only to products that could be profitable over the short-term. A number of new projects that had been worked on in connection with the evaporator were put aside. Only the projects that could reach a sales volume of at least $1 million in three years would be continued.

In the fall 1973, the oil crisis made the energy-intensive evaporator even harder to sell. The product line was discontinued and the technology sold to a division of White Consolidated in 1976. But the Lamella was beginning to emerge on the market in several different industry sectors. By the end of 1973, the product started covering its own costs. Parkson's manufacturing operation was moved to a new building in an industrial section of Pompano Beach, which allowed for expansion. During 1974 and especially

1975, sales of Lamella products increased considerably. Parkson was able to consolidate its finances, and started looking around for other equipment to extend its product line. But this change to a profitability came at the last minute; another six months of losses and Johnsons would have pulled out of its commitment.

The search for new products resulted in new licenses from the Axel Johnson Institute in Sweden. The next product was the Magnum Press, a machine for draining and pressing sludge into cakes. It was followed after a few years by the DynaSand Filter, a device for final treatment of wastewater before discharge.

In September 1979, which was financially a rather weak year for Parkson, Gustafsson was succeeded as president by G. Parks Souther. In a report to the New York company's board in April 1980, Souther defined Parkson's goals as building an operation based on technologically advanced products that provided yearly sales of $15 to $20 million and realizing steady returns of about 30 percent of invested capital. Investments in production resources would be kept down and subcontractors used to the greatest possible extent. Licenses would be sought for additional products. The company's organization would be restructured according to product lines, and each would be regarded as a profit center. At that point, Parkson had, as a whole, begun to show profits and pay back the investment of the parent company over the previous twelve years.

During the 1980s, new licenses were acquired. The liquid/solids product line was augmented with the Aqua Guard Screen, a device that separated incoming water from coarser material, the first step in the treatment process. The license to produce this unit was of Japanese origin. Another new product line, the Oxycharger, was acquired for the oxygenation of water. Additional licenses were bought in the 1980s from West Germany, Sweden (not the Axel Johnson Institute, however) and the United States. In 1985,

Parks Souther succeeded Carl Evert Gustafsson as president of Parkson in 1979. With 15 years in the position, he is the veteran among the presidents of the subsidiary companies.

Parkson bought the Endurex Corporation, a producer of diffusion devices. The idea behind these activities was to build the company's market share with products that had a very distinct competitive edge. The Lamella, for example, saved energy and space and was, therefore, easy to install in existing plants. As far as the self-cleaning filters of the DynaSand and Aqua Guard were concerned, the possibility of keeping them in continuous operation would be emphasized. Parkson showed, according to Souther, that it was possible to sell new cost-efficient technology even in a market that was quite conservative.

The Parkson business strategy proved succesful during the '80s. An exception was the recession year of 1983. Earnings increased three times, and after-tax return on capital was considerably higher than for Axel Johnson, Inc., as a whole. The story was, however, debated internally during the mid-1980s. John W. Priesing, who had succeeded Lynch as president of the New York company, indicated that Parkson during much of the 1970s had been a bad deal, »a dog«. Parks Souther was not slow with his response, stating his view of the company's progress:

> In summary, the '70s were necessary years if Parkson was going to survive and grow. I believe we did as well as could be expected under very difficult circumstances. Our long-range objective (or dream, really) was to build Parkson into the profitable market leader it is today. Certainly the profits we've made, plus the $25+ million the owner could now sell us for in the marketplace, has given her an outstanding return for Bob Lynch's and her father's patience and our efforts. Not bad for a 'dog'.«

Parkson's good performance resulted in the company being named the A. Johnson & Co., Inc., »Company of the Year« in 1985, 1986 and 1987. During that period, there were discussions of letting Parkson go public. Here the New York management saw the possibility of developing the kind of management incentives through stock option plans that were customary in U.S. business but difficult to establish in privately owned companies, and was strongly in favor of the move. The owner acknowledged the possible advantages but, in order to keep control, decided not to proceed. This profitable company should remain entirely in the family.

CHAPTER ELEVEN

Machines and metals

Robert Lynch's annual report from 1954 mentions »The Engineering and Trading Department« that »principally services our Swedish affiliates«. For the New York office in general, the old concept of being a small Swedish trading house in the United States, principally focused on Swedish exports and imports, had began to fall into the background. During the years immediately after World War II, trade policies were so unclear that the trading department of A. Johnson & Co., Inc., led an uncertain existence. In the beginning of the 1950s though, volume picked up again.

In 1954, the department consisted of two metallurgists, an import/export man, a salesman and a secretary. From 1958 on, it was known as the »Industrial Sales Department«. All through the '50s, it sold ferrochromium, stainless steel piping and brewing equipment from Avesta, electrolytic iron powder from Husqvarna and stainless steel cutlery from Motala. Besides supplying other types of stainless steel equipment to South America and Formosa, the department also bought ship plate for Lindholmen, chemicals for the Malmö office, coal for A. Johnson & Co HAB and nickel for Avesta.

The Industrial Sales Department also made inquiries – on behalf of the Johnson companies – into cold-rolled steel technology, titanium manufacture and off-shore techniques, and investigated the possibilities of shipping methane gas and collaborating with Westinghouse on the development of atomic power. The department performed market studies to see if licenses could be sold for various items of the Johnson Group repertoire, for example, Avesta-Karrer's drier and other equipment for the paper pulp industry.

There had been plans for broader activity within the industrial sales area. In the early 1950s, Axel Ax:son Johnson Jr. suggested that the company could be the U.S. agents for Kamyr, similar to the arrangement in France where A.Johnson & Cie represented this Scandinavian joint venture. Kamyr had been created by KMW of Sweden, Myhrens Verksteder of Norway and Karhula of Finland in order to exploit an innovation in the paper pulp industry, namely the continuous boiling process. But the Norwegian partner opposed these plans, arguing that although in France Johnsons was merely a marketing agency, in North America it would be a question of manufacturing under licence. Therefore, Kamyr ought to set up its own organization there. It was already represented by Paper Machinery Ltd. (PML), which had a manufacturing agreement with Sandy Hill Iron & Brass Works, Hudson Falls, New York. These two were taken in as minor partners in the new corporation, Kamyr, Inc. On financial and practical matters, the new firm cooperated with A.Johnson & Co., Inc., and Axel Ax:son Johnson Jr. became chairman of the board.

The establishment of Kamyr, Inc., deprived the New York firm of a potential market. So did the decision to establish a Johnson office in Canada. There had been a shipping office in Vancouver, C. Gardner Johnson, since the 1930s. In the early 1950s, Axel Ax:son Johnson Jr. started planning for a new office in eastern Canada, »to represent mainly Karlstad, Avesta, but also other workshops ... investment in oil and minerals and manufacturing facilities included in long-range program ...«

A.Johnson & Co. (Canada) Ltd. was incorporated in 1956 in

Montreal, under the auspices of A. Johnson & Co., Inc. The concept was very much the same as in New York. The company was engaged in the manufacturing and marketing of water turbines, the storage of stainless steel for Avesta and the construction business, drawing on Swedish experience using concrete piling in swampy areas. Lynch was a member of the board of the Canadian firm, which eventually, in the mid-1980s was purchased by the New York company. That process was, in a way, parallel to what happened with the San Francisco office.

In 1965, A. Johnson & Co HAB, as sole owners, set up an office in San Francisco to market products from Avesta and Karlstads Mekaniska Verkstad. The company was called A. Johnson & Co., Inc. (Calif.). There are any number of possible reasons why the Swedish company chose to sidestep the New York company. The managers of the New York company were not interested in marketing steel and paper machinery and declined to open up an affiliate office at the West Coast. HAB, on the other hand, strongly felt there was an obligation in the Group strategy to distribute the Group's products all over the United States, wherever there seemed to be a market.

As president of the new company, Börje Wahlström, KMW's technical director, was put in charge of sales of KMW's products. Gunnar Dandanell was recruited from the Montreal office to manage steel sales. However, the firm did not thrive, and the New York company was obliged to take over its operations. Thus, in 1969, a special department for paper and paper-pulp processing machines was established in New York as a result of the San Francisco venture's collapse. Six staff members were relocated from San Francisco to Bala Cynwyd in Philadelphia, among them Börje Wahlström, who at the same time was named vice president of A. Johnson & Co., Inc. During the first year, this department did indeed manage to sell a couple of paper machines, but continued to lose money. The department was offered a number of opportunities to bid but lost the lot: KMW's prices were too high, and its payment terms too rigorous. Still another problem was KMW's late deliveries. In 1971, the New York company was accused of dumping in connection with a sale made to a company in Oklahoma. The subsequent lawsuit in 1973 was settled favorably. A simple oversight in billing was judged to have caused the low price.

Agencies and licenses for different types of equipment were now acquired from the Axel Johnson Institute and from Motala Mekaniska Verkstad, another company in the Johnson Group that produced presses for fiber construction board. In spite of a few sales, there were losses all through 1972 and the years that followed. The market was sluggish, and the recession in the construction sector caused the Motala business to slump. In 1976, the department was disbanded and its operations moved to a new company, KMW-Johnson, Inc., which was 50 percent owned by A. Johnson & Co., Inc., and 50 percent by KMW. Charlotte, North Carolina, was the site of the new offshoot. The business concept was to market equipment for the paper industry that would be manufactured in part by KMW in Sweden, in part by subcontractors in the United States, and finally assembled by KMW-Johnson, Inc. The New York company, however, soon pulled out of the venture – which progressed rather poorly – and sold its share to KMW.

The dealings in iron powder also deserve a more detailed explanation. In 1952, A. Johnson & Co., Inc., had begun selling iron powder for Husqvarna, a Swedish engineering corporation. The Chrysler Corporation was reported to be planning to buy all the iron powder that could be supplied. Iron powder could be pressed into light engine parts. For a few years, the company considered manufacturing engine parts of its own, but the Johnson Group management in Sweden put a stop to that idea. Instead, the company began marketing a Belgian press and a Swedish grinding machine. The business grew, more personnel were employed and in 1960 a laboratory was set up in Newark, New Jersey. Besides Sweden, iron powder was imported from Italy. A warehouse on Long Island was rented for storing the powder and demonstrating the machines.

Soon this business had grown to be the most important source of income for the Industrial Sales Department. New suppliers were sought. A powder developed by the Swedish company Stora Kopparberg was tested. Some collaboration began between the two companies, but was cancelled after a couple of years. In 1965, the department began selling Japanese powder. A new production process was developed by Avesta, in which a General Motors subcontractor showed interest.

In 1967, however, a new quality of iron powder, »atomized powder«, appeared on the market, at half the price of the electrolytic powder that A. Johnson & Co., Inc., offered. The New York company had, in fact, advised Motala to start manufacturing powder according to the new method, but without success. The firm could no longer compete, and in 1969 the whole operation was sold to Höganäs in Riverton, New Jersey. The warehouse in Newark was closed, but the laboratory equipment was moved to a new department of A. Johnson & Co., Inc., called SKC and located in Hawthorne, New Jersey, and the operation was reorganized.

In 1970, a license was acquired from the Axel Johnson Institute in Nynäshamn, Sweden, to recondition tungsten for use in rock drill crowns, a relatively untried process at the time. This project, which was run in collaboration with the U.S. firm Mallory, was planned as a long-term operation. The department built a factory in Kentucky and signed a contract with Kamyr, Inc., to run it. Production difficulties plagued the factory, however, and experts from the Institute could not rectify the situation. With the market falling off, the department ran at a loss, and in 1975 the business was finally phased out as Mallory withdrew.

In 1969, the steel business run by Johnsons in San Francisco (see page 171) was taken over by a newly established Steel Division of the New York company. Storage and marketing remained located in San Francisco and Philadelphia. For various reasons, political as well as economic, the division's losses continued during the first few years of the '70s. Soon though, the business changed course. It was no longer considered important to approach end users; instead, distributors were to be targeted. The warehouse in San Francisco was shut down, and the shearing equipment installed in Philadelphia was sold. New sales offices were opened in Houston and Chicago. A purchasing department was set up to supply Avesta with scrap iron and aluminum. For all intents and purposes, the manner in which the New York company ran Avesta's agency was a return to its business concept from the interwar years.

Sales of stainless steel increased in 1972. Losses became earnings. But this good luck was short-lived. The company was accused of dumping, which triggered a comprehensive investigation of Avesta's prices. The question of whether or not product was dumped was determined by the level of prices in the goods' country of origin, not by the world market price. The burden of proof was on the accused, i.e., companies were presumed guilty unless they could present evidence to the contrary. In Lynch's opinion, Avesta had only itself to blame; through the Swedish Ironmasters Association (Jernkontoret) the company had formed a de facto cartel that had rigged prices so high in Sweden that it fell into its own trap. In

1973, a conviction was handed down by the court, threatening heavy fines if the imports continued.

The dumping conviction caused deliveries of stainless steel from Avesta to fall off dramatically, but the slack was taken up by imports of Japanese sheet metal. Needless to say, this affected Johnsons' interests in Sweden. But Axel Ax:son Johnson argued that if he could not export sheet metal from Sweden, he could manufacture it in the United States. »Get me a steel mill!« were his orders. The search and negotiations began. Lynch was loyal, but did not share the owner's interest or enthusiasm for the venture.

The steel mill in New Castle, Indiana, was founded in 1899 as the Indiana Rolling Mills Company. In 1917, it was purchased by Stephen A. Ingersoll, who sold it twelve years later to the steel concern Borg-Warner. In 1975, the company's management bought out the three steel divisions of Borg-Warner to found BW Steel. One year later, this company sold the rather antiquated mill for hot-rolled and special steels to A. Johnson & Co., Inc. Across the street, the more modern factory for cold-rolled steel was acquired by one of Avesta's competitors, Allegheny-Ludlum.

The Johnson purchase of Ingersoll Steel Company was announced in Sweden in connection with the 1976 opening of Avesta's new wide-strip rolling mill. The official reason for the move was the protectionism that Avesta had faced in the United States, in the form of dumping penalties as well as import quotas, which had forced Avesta's exports down from a potential 8,000 tons a year to 2,000 to 3,000 tons. The intention was to produce stainless steel and manufacture farming tools, for example, saw-blades and plowshares. Besides stainless, the Indiana mill produced certain mild steels.

From the beginning, the company ran at a loss due to the slump in the industry at large, inadequate stocks, which prevented it from seizing sales opportunities, and its need for overall renovation. Over the years, large investments were made: The wide strip was broadened and X-ray analysis was installed, as well as a new converter. Stocks were increased.

In 1978, the company was incorporated, for tax purposes, into the Steel Division of A. Johnson & Co., Inc., and its name was changed to Ingersoll Johnson Steel Company. Although reorganization and modernization of its operations were effected that first year, the results were disappointing. Analysis revealed that still another line of products was necessary: milled tool steel. Towards the end of the year, the steel market took an upswing and losses decreased. During 1979, the company began making money although its investments were still not producing a return. But the company was holding its own, and production of steel plate grew rapidly. As far as plowshares were concerned, Ingersoll dominated the U.S. market completely.

A sweeping change of leadership was carried out at Ingersoll; a young team with a high level of technical competence supplanted the old guard. New collective-wage agreements were negotiated with employees, but – according to unanimous testimony – union opposition made it very difficult to modify the existing labor organization; for some obscure reason, most of the work force were members of the United Autoworkers' Union. During the first transitional period, the Swede Erik Berg served as president. He was succeeded in 1977 by T. Grant John.

In the beginning of the 1980s, Ingersoll's business began slumping again. Rigidity in the organization made it hard to trim the company to conform to new market demands. The management in New York wanted to shut down the mill and offset the loss with earnings from the oil trade. At that juncture, HAB's president, Göran Ennerfelt, offered to buy Ingersoll to use the mill as an asset

The Ingersoll steel mill in New Castle, Indiana, was acquired in order to replace import of steel from Avesta with import of Swedish production technology.

in the negotiations with other producers in Sweden that were being conducted under government supervision in 1982–83 and resulted in a strong concentration of the Swedish specialty steel business. Thus, Ingersoll was sold to HAB, which in turn transferred the company to the new Swedish specialty steel concern, Avesta AB. Ingersoll later became a valuable asset to that company, which since 1995 is entirely owned by British interests.

Richard (Dick) Sandquist, left, started Johnsons' titanium business. Here he is sorting titanium scrap in Finland in 1984.

In the early 1970s, the raw materials department of the Steel Division bought scrap nickel for Avesta, as well as scrap titanium and ferrotitanium for itself. In 1973, this business developed further. The entrepreneur was Richard (Dick) Sandquist, an American of Scandinavian descent. He started buying scrap titanium in the Soviet Union – usually through a British middleman – for delivery to the American market. Prices were incredibly low and good profits could be made. In 1974, a small factory was set up in Downingtown, Pennsylvania, where this scrap could be sorted – the old way, by hand – and processed, and where the necessary laboratory tests could be carried out. In 1975, modern X-ray equipment was installed for metal analysis. Imports from the Soviet Union were successively replaced by metals from other sources, for example, Red China, and by local materials.

Carlos Aguirre, president of Axel Johnson Metals until 1993, and Antonia
Ax:son Johnson.

A special division, the Industrial Metals Division, was established in February 1977, including a trading department, a welding
department and a raw materials department. The last two were
housed in new factories in Lionville, Pennsylvania. Ken McAlpine,
a lawyer whose main experience was gained in the Johnson oil business, was hired as manager. The titanium trade, which accounted
for about 20 percent of the American market, did rather well, but
earnings were eroded by the welding department's losses. Eventually, the welding department became a retail outlet and was sold to
Avesta. The scrap recycling and trading business became less profitable in the early 1980s. The metals trading business was sold in
1986 to Axore, a business unit in the Swedish Johnson Group. The
titanium business seemed more promising, and the decision was
made to integrate downstream.

In 1981, Howard Harker, a consulting engineer, was hired to design an electron beam furnace for melting down titanium scrap and turnings into slabs or ingots of titanium and titanium alloys for use in high-performance applications. Electron guns were imported from East Germany, a deal in which A. Johnson & Co HAB played a role. The furnace was built in a new factory in Morgantown, Pennsylvania, not far from Lionsville. A metallurgist, Carlos Aguirre, was recruited from Ingersoll to head the Industrial Metals Division, which was incorporated as Axel Johnson Metals, Inc., in 1984.

Titanium is used in the aircraft industry, in jet engines and frames, because it combines strength with light weight and resistance to heat and corrosion. Using its own patented refining process, specified by General Electric, a leading jet engine manufacturer, Axel Johnson Metals became dominant in that market. The company was also serving chemical, pulp and paper and other processors in the industrial market.

Construction began in 1988 on a second, bigger and more sophisticated electron beam furnace, which was scheduled to begin operation in 1990. The new furnace provided Axel Johnson Metals with the increased production capacity needed to confront the sharper competition of the 1990s.

CHAPTER TWELVE

Restructuring

DuRING THE ALMOST 30 YEARS that Robert Lynch was president of A. Johnson & Co., Inc., the company was transformed and developed in almost every respect. The tiny office in New York with a handful of employees of the early 1950s had become a corporate headquarters with subsidiaries spread over the United States, mainly along the East Coast, by the early 1980s. It was no longer »our man in New York«, it was an industrial concern in its own right.

Size in itself provided the basis for more self-confidence vis-à-vis the Swedish Johnson Group. But vital, and in this respect perhaps more important, was also the fact that the red bottom line in the annual reports had turned black. Financially, there had been a shift from losses to profits in the U.S. business, from time to time even large profits, which of course gave the U.S. management greater freedom of action. The figures are given in Appendix 1, table 2.

Earning money did not mean that the management in New York could make independent decisions on strategy, but it gave some leeway. Earning money provided funds for investment and credibility for borrowing from the banks. The policy adopted by the owner was that all U.S. business investments should be paid for by the U.S. company and all necessary borrowing should be done in the United States on the basis of the business credibility of the New

York company, not the Johnson Group in Sweden or elsewhere. This strategy was adhered to except, as shown in Chapter 9, in the case of the Sprague purchase.

During the early years, profits were made primarily in shipping, where some long-term contracts generated a fairly good income and provided a firm foundation for the whole U.S. business of Johnsons. Later that role was taken over by the oil trade, which especially during the turbulent 1970s generated amounts of money virtually unheard of in the history of the company.

The profits generated in shipping and oil were invested in rather traditional manufacturing businesses, Bird-Johnson and Parkson, which both took off by exploiting innovations from the Swedish Group in the United States, the KaMeWa propeller and the Lamella separator. On the Swedish owners' side, there was always a certain cautiousness or even reluctance to invest heavily in industrial plants and equipment. A subcontractor approach was favored at the beginning in both Massachusetts and Florida, but as business developed, production was transferred to the companies' own premises. During the 1970s, due to growth in size and the availability of funds, more and more capital was invested in plants and heavy equipment in Fort Lauderdale, South Walpole and elsewhere, not least in the steel mill in New Castle, Indiana.

A. Johnson & Co., Inc., had matured and started to form a family of its own. And that family bore a striking similarity to the family from which it sprang. In a way, the corporation evolved into a U.S. version of the Swedish Johnson Group, in which Bird-Johnson was the KMW, Parkson was the Motala, Sprague the Nynäs, Ingersoll the Avesta, the Panamanian companies the Nordstjernan and the office in Manhattan the equivalent of the Group central office at Stureplan, Stockholm.

The hierarchial structure within A. Johnson & Co., Inc., was built

Robert M. Lynch was president and CEO of A. Johnson & Co., Inc., from 1953 to 1981. During his era, the telephone became the most important means of communication within the company and between the owner and the president.

up with the corporate head office in New York and separate management teams at the subsidiaries, Bird-Johnson, Parkson, Sprague and Ingersoll.

The company had already begun organizing operations into divisions during the 1950s. Divisionalization was then a current trend in management; the New York company did what many companies did at the time. Later, in the early 1980s, divisions were incorporated as separate companies, like the Oil Division, which became Axel Johnson Energy Corporation, and the Industrial Metals Division, which became Axel Johnson Metals, Inc. This resulted in a more clear-cut corporate structure.

The subsidiaries operated within the guidelines of a three-year plan, an annual budget and a yearly financial report, all of which had to be approved by corporate management. They could make maintenance investments at their own discretion, but for new investments approval had to be sought from New York. It was a fairly centralized structure, much in the paternalistic tradition of the Johnsons.

All along, the relationship with the Swedish owner and the Swedish industrial operations remained close. Neither the right nor the competence of Axel Ax:son Johnson to participate in the business and make the ultimate decisions were ever disputed, though Lynch in specific cases might have held and voiced another opinion. But the president was very loyal to his chairman, and the kind of difficulties that had been so frequent between Wilkens and the Consul General never disturbed their relationship. Axel Ax:son Johnson continued to spend a lot of time in the United States and liked it there. In fact, many of his formative experiences, both as a businessman and as a private person, occurred in the United States. He met his wife and formed his own family in America. He understood far better than his more Europe-minded father the conditions of life and business in America.

Nevertheless, there was never any doubt about the »Swedishness« of the New York company. At the headquarters and also in the subsidiaries, Swedes were often appointed to important positions; there was an exhange of personnel between the Johnson companies in Sweden and the U.S. companies, which was facilitated by the structural similarity of the businesses.

When the leader of a patriarchal organization dies, there will either be an appointed heir to the throne or there will be a more or less open fight for power. But when he is merely disabled, there is often no clear successor to take the lead. In February 1975, Axel Ax:son Johnson was struck by a cerebral haemorrhage from which he never fully recovered, although he resumed some of his duties after a few months.

The arrangements made for the succession of power within the family had not taken into consideration the possibility of a handicapped leader. The situation could be contrasted with that in the mid-1950s, when the Consul General became steadily less able to provide leadership due to his age. His son gradually grew into the role of leader. When the old man died in August 1958, the management transition was smooth. In 1975, however, no successor was immediately in readiness.

Axel Ax:son Johnson had one child, Antonia. She was born in 1943 in New York and spent her first nine years there, with the exception of 1944–46. In 1953 the family returned to Sweden, where she grew up. After finishing secondary school Antonia Ax:son Johnson spent her junior year at Radcliffe college in Cambridge, Massachussets. Back home again, she married Nils Mörner, the president of a firm that later became an affiliate of the Johnson Group. Within ten years, she had a family of four children. Starting in 1964 she studied – part-time – economics and psychology at the Stockholm University. She graduated in 1971 after having spent two years in the United States working with Citibank and Bank of America. At the time of her father's stroke, Antonia was working in the Personnel Department of the Johnson Group, still not in any prominent position. The plan was for her to take over in due time, but being at the beginning of her business career, she was not ready to assume leadership in 1975.

During the first stages of Axel Ax:son Johnson's illness, his intentions and wishes were interpreted by a small circle of close associates, a temporary arrangement in order to keep business going with a minimum of disruption. By summer 1975, Johnson had returned to working part-time, and his associates tried to arrange his sur-

Axel Ax:son Johnson's most important and closest advisor was his wife, Antonia, who often accompanied him on his journeys around the world. Mrs. Johnson survived her husband by five years.

roundings so that his physical handicaps would trouble him as little as possible. For four years, he continued to carry out his various functions as before, including international travel, although his strength gradually began to fail.

At Nordstjernan, where all the Johnson siblings were shareholders, in the autumn of 1978, four executive vice presidents were appointed to help out, a tactic that served its purpose in terms of work flow but not in terms of strategic vision or clear leadership. In late summer 1979, Johnson was persuaded by his closest advisors to relinquish his position. He was succeeded as president of the shipping company by his brother, Bo Ax:son Johnson. Bo had been president of the Nynäs refinery for a long time and had thus specialized in the oil business. Though he had served on the board of some of the companies and of the family foundations, he had not been closely involved in the strategic concerns of the Johnson Group.

The situation was different in A. Johnson & Co HAB, where Axel Ax:son Johnson was the sole owner. There he was replaced by Göran Ennerfelt as president. After spending his junior year at Williams College in Williamstown, Massachusetts, Ennerfelt graduated from the Stockholm School of Economics and Stockholm University. Working at the Institute for East European Studies, he was taken on by Axel Johnson in 1964 as a personal assistant. He held that position for five years, and then made a career within A. Johnson & Co. On a personal level, Ennerfelt remained close to Axel A:son Johnson, regardless of the fact that other personal assistants were appointed after him.

The ailing Axel Ax:son Johnson remained chairman of the board of both companies until 1981, when he was succeeded on Nordstjernan's board by his brother, and 1982, when his daughter, Antonia Ax:son Johnson, took over as chairman of the board of A. Johnson & Co HAB.

Robert M. Lynch, here with his wife Jinx, was awarded the Swedish Order of Vasa for his long and successful service to Swedish business interests in the United States.

The effect of these leadership changes was that the Johnson Group began to split up. The trading firm, A. Johnson & Co HAB, had been linked to the rest of the group through a personal union, to describe the situation in dynastic terms. Now Nordstjernan and its affiliates were run by Bo Ax:son Johnson, chairman, and Rune Hallåker, president, while Antonia Ax:son Johnson's role in its affairs diminished.

Major changes were in store for the Group. A shift in management at Nordstjernan in 1985 represented a drastic break with tradition and with the strategic idea that until then had guided the business of Johnsons: staying private, acquiring companies when needed as a complement to other businesses or when a good opportunity arose, but seldom divesting. Now came a radical restructuring of the group, a concentration to a small number of core businesses and a very conscious divesting of many of the older companies. In a couple of years, the Johnson conglomerate was turned into one of Sweden's largest construction firms, under the name of NCC, Nordic Construction Company AB.

The 1980s and the first part of the '90s were also turbulent years for A. Johnson & Co HAB, with a rapid series of changes both in the structure of the organization and in the lines of business. In 1988, the company's name was changed to Axel Johnson AB. Through a series of acquisitions and divestitures, the company went out of oil refining and oil trading as well as ore and metals trading and concentrated its activities in four core business areas: retailing and wholesaling of food, importation and distribution of fruit and vegetables, department stores, and international trade, primarily in industrial semiconsumables. Most of the new business areas were predominantly Swedish or Scandinavian in orientation and also consumer oriented. This was a shift from the former concentration on industrial trading in international markets.

The U.S. corporation had started its restructuring earlier. The basic business rationale had been found elsewhere. Now, the dramatic structural change in the Johnson Group in Sweden emphazised that the old model was no longer there. The tight links between the Swedish and American companies were no longer as natural as they had been before.

For A. Johnson & Co., Inc., Axel Ax:son Johnson's illness meant that the patriarch was no longer able to lead with his customary strength. The fact that Mr. Johnson was spending more and more time in Naples, Florida, did not mean much in that respect. From 1979 on, his friend Ernest Arbuckle, who was a member of the board, served as the owner's representative vis-à-vis management, an arrangement that did not delight the president, Robert Lynch. The collaboration between Johnson and Lynch was built on a solid base of personal loyalty and friendship. »We thought a lot alike,« said Lynch, »we seldom surprised each other.« That Lynch positioned himself so close to his chairman makes it hard to assess the exact nature of their collaboration and to distribute criticism and credit for actions taken. It seems, however, as if Johnson was the one who took initiatives and declared his intentions, while Lynch was the keen listener and the expedient doer.

Towards the end of the 1970s, Lynch was approaching retirement. »Operation Abraham Lincoln« was the code name for the search to find a new president. In 1977, John W. Priesing, who was a group vice president and director of Phelps Dodge Industries and had a background in consulting and metals processing, was signed on. In 1978, he became executive vice president, directly responsible for the manufacturing companies. In 1981, he took charge as president and chief executive officer of A. Johnson & Co., Inc.

But the changes were not just in the personnel of the New York office. The business concept, which was still in force, called for the U.S. company to represent the Johnson Group and its affiliates in the world market. Now, in the beginning of the 1980s, the Group in the old sense was gradually falling apart, and some of those companies, like Avesta, longed to be free to choose their own representation in the United States. Therefore, the important assignment was to develop A. Johnson & Co., Inc., into a more independent U.S. corporation – a thought, incidentally, that Axel Ax:son Johnson had nurtured but was never able to bring to fruition. Now the opportunity was there. As a result of the exceptional oil profits, es-

John Priesing, with his background in manufacturing and consulting, was recruited to A. Johnson & Co., Inc., to lead the company away from its heavy dependence on oil and into other business sectors.

pecially in 1979, the New York company's coffers were full. By investing in new companies and divesting of old ones, it was thought, the company could renew itself and develop businesses that were not based on oil. For that task, John Priesing was taken on.

Lynch gave two specific pieces of advice to his successor. First, divest the oil refining business, and second, don't lose the money earned during the incredible days of oil trading. It was a rather conservative policy that the former president recommended to John Priesing. So was, in fact, the aquisition policy that the board adopted. During the following few years, a number of purchases were made. Priesing's requirements were that any company bought should cost no more than $30 to 35 million, and that external financing of each deal should not exceed 45 percent of the total capital investment. In addition, any company purchased had to show a positive return on the invested capital after three years at the most. It did not matter very much what industry sector a company was in as long as it met these requirements, although there was some focus on electronics.

Priesing saw this as a cautious strategy. This view is, in a way, supported by A. George Gebauer, who together with Cameron Caswell formed the company's acquisition group. In a later interview, Gebauer claimed that if its leaders had disregarded their ethical standards, Axel Johnson & Co., Inc., could have launched a far more aggressive acquisition policy. These were the golden days of the the »junk bond« business of the 1980s, and the »leveraged buyout« was a common a way of financing large purchases through substantial borrowing. Within the established strategy, there were, of course – in hindsight – missed opportunities and mistakes, as well as purchases that turned out well.

ITI (Industrial Tectronics, Inc.), in Michigan, was bought in 1982. The company manufactured high-precision balls and ball- and roller-bearings for the machine and instrument industry. ITI, which cost some $20 million to buy, had a good cash flow but yielded only modest earnings. The purchase was accompanied by a host of problems in connection with an earlier federal contract, making it a disastrous experience for A. Johnson & Co., Inc.

A far more successful investment was the purchase in June 1983 of *Hekimian Laboratories, Inc.,* in Maryland. The company, producing test equipment for the telecommunications industry, cost $42 million. At the end of 1987, the New York company bought *Larse Corporation*, California, for $13.3 million. The aquisition was part of a long-term strategy to build up strength in the telecommunications industry. Larse was initially seen as a complement to Hekimian, though the similarities turned out not to be so synergetic. (cf. Chapter 13.)

As complements to Sprague, *S&S-Hartwell & Co., Inc.,* a heating oil and gasoline wholesaler, and a bulk oil terminal in Maine were

ITI manufactured, among other things, precision balls from many different materials in many sizes for use in a variety of industrial and consumer products.

bought, all in December 1987. These purchases, which cost $1.6 million, were also successful.

Some subsidiaries were both purchased and sold during the 1980s. The *IDE Corporation*, which was bought in December 1985 for $22 million – the founders retained a 10 percent equity position – manufactured peripheral equipment mainly for IBM personal computers. The business did not develop as expected. The type of equipment the company made was soon incorporated into computers at the assembly stage. There also turned out to be some unforeseen management problems in dealing with the founders of the company. In the beginning, Priesing had been quite impressed with this group, but he was never able to establish a good rapport with them. Cultural differencies may have played a role. The company was sold at the beginning of 1988, resulting in a gain of approximately $1 million, although the overall position resulted in a loss. In 1985, a minority holding was bought in *Aries Electronics, Inc.*, for $11 million. Aries manufactured switchgear for the electronics industry. It was sold back to its previous owners in 1990 without any significant loss. The economic returns while it was part of the company had been small.

Some purchases belong to a special category. They do not fit the acquisition strategy for the U.S. company; the rationale has to be sought elsewhere. Here we are dealing with purchases from A. Johnson & Co HAB. *A. Johnson (Canada) Inc.*, formerly *Brian Engineering Ltd.*, was bought from the Swedish firm in January 1985 in order to increase managerial control over this affiliate of the Group. The company manufactured and distributed instruments for the processing industry and marketed Parkson's devices for treating industrial wastewater and sewage. A similar motive, as well as financial reasons, were behind the acquisitions of *Axel Johnson Corporation* with its subsidiary *Axel Johnson Engineering Corporation*, an engineering company specialized in hydroelectric power stations. These purchases cost the company around $1 million.

Purchasing is not the only way to expand. New operations could also be started up from scratch. In 1986, *Axel Johnson Cogeneration, Inc.*, (later *A. Johnson Energy Development, Inc.*) started the first two of a series of alternate energy projects at the cost of about $18 million. The idea was to take advantage of political incentives to produce alternate energy in joint ventures with local consumers of energy. For different reasons, some of which could have been foreseen while others were more difficult to anticipate, the project developed over the years into a real problem child for Axel Johnson Inc. Only after lengthy processes, including law suits, was it possible to get out of this failed venture. Losses were substantial.

A. Johnson & Co., Inc., was thoroughly transformed during the 1980s. At the beginning of the decade, 80 percent of its earnings came from the oil business. By the time its name was changed in 1988 to Axel Johnson Inc., Priesing had succeeded in making it a diversified industrial corporation with businesses spread all over North America and the oil business representing just 12 percent. The aquisitions in the telecommunications industry turned out to be especially important.

The wide range of operations gave corporate headquarters a new strategic role. The subsidiaries still operated on a budget basis, decided at the corporate level. Finance was centralized and all external borrowing was negotiated through corporate headquarters in order to get the most favorable terms. The company no longer bore any similarities to its Swedish sister and was not representing Swedish producers' interests in the U.S. market. It was an American corporation, and the fact that it was Swedish owned had no great importance. The identification with the Johnson family and its long tradition was weakened as the company grew by acquiring subsidiaries in new fields. There was no longer any strong, common corporate culture in A. Johnson & Co., Inc., and its subsidiaries.

John Priesing was an energetic, operations-oriented manager with clearly defined demands for performance and order in the organization. He tried to increase coordination between the various divisions and subsidiaries by introducing yearly »presidents' meetings« – originally suggested by the chairman – and demanding more disciplined reporting to the New York head office, never directly to the owner. Still – and perhaps because of the clash between this slightly bureaucratic, managerial professionalism and a more paternalistic management style in the Johnson tradition – he and the Swedish leaders started to grate on each other.

Priesing was convinced that no company could be run from a distance. He was clearly committed to turning the New York office into a concern with a distinctly American identity. His critics viewed him as alien, almost antipathetic to the company's Swedish heritage. That a subsidiary should report directly to the owner – as for example C.E. Gustafsson tried as president of Parkson in the 1970s – was beyond question. It might be worthwhile to note that the principle established by the Consul General and strictly adhered to by his son – i.e., that the treasurer in the U.S. firm must always be a Swede – was abandoned in 1980 when Stig Sultan stepped down and no Swede was found to succeed him. Geoff Magrath got the job and the New York management became more »Americanized«.

At the beginning of his tenure, Priesing did not feel the influence of a powerful owner in the sense that his predecessors had. Both Wilkens and Lynch had met a patriarch, older than themselves, with a strong industrial position in his own country and an explicit authority in the New York office. Priesing, on the other hand, met Antonia Ax:son Johnson in the early stage of her career as chairman of the company. He was older and experienced at the job and perceived her as inexperienced. Priesing took a somewhat paternalistic attitude toward the new chairman, which in time diminished the prospects for a good working relationship. The president of A. Johnson & Co HAB, Göran Ennerfelt, who also sat on the Board of Directors of the New York company, was perceived by Priesing as a spearhead for asserting the Swedish companies' interests. Ennerfelt's special relation to the owner of A. Johnson & Co., Inc. – he married Antonia Ax:son Johnson in 1984 – added to the communication problems.

However, the difficulty cannot be reduced to a question of personal chemistry, though that was an important factor. There was an obvious rift between the owner and the management in their way of

Göran Ennerfelt, president and
CEO of Axel Johnson AB since
1979, and a board member of Axel
Johnson Inc. In 1984 he married
Antonia Ax:son Johnson.

assessing certain business issues. Coordination in the international oil market was one area of contention, as was the value of Bird-Johnson and Sprague. The problem purchases, like ITI and IDE and the cogeneration projects, were other sources of friction. Allocating responsibility for the bad investments became, in itself, a source of disunity between the parties.

Modest financial results, shrinking tangible worth and increasing goodwill were key subjects of dispute and would gradually erode credibility between the management and the board of the company.

There were also different opinions about how to use the financial resources of the company. As a rule since the late 1940s, profits generated by the U.S. company were plowed back into the operations instead of being sent back to Sweden. When profits increased, token dividends were taken out to satisfy the Swedish Currency office (see Chapter 5). In 1987 and 1988, however, the board decided on a new policy, and much larger dividends were now paid, about twenty times the usual sum. The board's stated objective was to exert normal financial pressure on the company by draining off excessive capital. Priesing, however, having proposed a more ambitious growth strategy, viewed the owner's decision as an expression of no confidence. He also suspected that the dividends were a way to allow the U.S. corporation to help out at a time when Axel Johnson AB was under financial pressure in Sweden, something which, in his view, the board of the U.S. firm, obliged as it was to give top priority to the interests of Axel Johnson Inc., should not do.

Priesing's suspicion was repudiated by the owner. No large sums were transferred to Sweden; instead, the dividends were allocated to her personal holding company in the United States, Lexa, and were principally available for investments in Axel Johnson Inc. if that was needed and considered a good alternative. From the beginning, Lexa had been a subsidiary company to A. Johnson & Co., Inc., established in order to make it possible to give management some equity. A similar function was earlier to be filled by a company called Titan Petroleum, Inc. The idea of having side companies in order to let managers in privately held corporations be compensated with stock options was inspired by the way this was arranged at the Ford corporation. Lexa, however, was reorganized in 1985 when parent company and subsidiary shifted their positions.

It does seem likely that the U.S. enterprise »saved« some of the Swedish company's unsuccesful investments in the United States, like the San Fransisco business in the 1970s and the Canadian firm in the '80s, although both were consummated on an »arm's-length's basis«. In that way, the U.S. company supported the Swedish. It also seems clear that liquid assets from Lexa, generated in the United States, were in fact transferred into Swedish assets some years later. To what extent that was the case falls aside of the scope of this study.

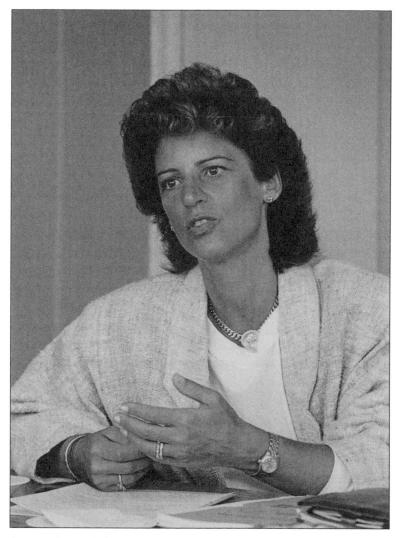

Antonia Ax:son Johnson in the mid-1980s. She evolved into a strong
and active owner and chairman of A. Johnson & Co., Inc., maybe to
the surprise of the CEO of the time.

Ernest Arbuckle, dean of the Stanford Graduate School of Business, and his wife Katherine (Kitty), were personal friends of Axel Ax:son Johnson and his family. Arbuckle served during different periods as a board member of A. Johnson & Co., Inc., and as a trustee of Bird-Johnson. The Arbuckles, here portrayed by C. Ryan, died in an automobile accident in 1986.

The relationship between the president and the chairman of the board gradually became intolerable. Ernest Arbuckle, who together with Robert Lynch had been largely responsible for recruiting John Priesing, acted as a kind of moderator between the contenders. When he died in a car crash at the outset of 1986, the antagonism between the owning family and Priesing became impossible to bridge.

As early as 1984, Arbuckle had contacted Vernon R. Anderson, a telecommunications consultant and contractor based in Silicon Valley, to offer him membership on the Board of Directors of the New York firm. Anderson hesitated, but accepted the post after a meet-

Vernon Anderson, a Californian enterpreneur, served as vice chairman of the company's board from 1988 to 1993 and was instrumental in solving the management crisis at Axel Johnson Inc. He was interim president and CEO from 1988 to 1989 and remained chairman of the board's Executive Committee until 1994.

ing with Antonia Ax:son Johnson and Göran Ennerfelt in late autumn 1985. During 1986, board meetings were held with unusual frequency, which gave Anderson a good insight into the company. He gained the confidence of the owner. He found faults with Priesing's investments, as well as the structure of the corporate group. It had become too fragmented, he felt, and the company did not have sufficient competence in the areas where investments had been made. A. Johnson & Co., Inc., should be concentrating on telecommunications and environmental technology, was Anderson's advice. Also, in making acquisitions, more emphasis should be placed on the potentials for earnings, growth and a strong balance sheet.

During the course of 1987, Vernon Anderson was increasingly seen by the owner to be a person she could enroll in the transformation of the firm's management that she desired. He had an old family connection to Sweden and a close friendship with Arbuckle. More important however, was his experience as a high-technology entrepreneur and executive, who had founded and built up three different corporations and restructured a number of others. In January 1988, Antonia Ax:son Johnson and Vernon Anderson had a lengthy meeting in Florida at which a new plan of operations was drawn up. Anderson was assigned to implement it. In March, he was named vice chairman of the board and chairman of the executive committee. John Priesing, who thus became a »lame duck«, resigned in September and was granted an early retirement effective the middle of October 1988. He was succeeded as chief executive officer by Vernon Anderson – a temporary arrangement until a successor was appointed.

CHAPTER THIRTEEN

Telecommunications

TELECOMMUNICATIONS – especially merged with computers
– is a rapidly growing industry in the United States and worldwide.
In the early 1980s, when A. Johnson & Co., Inc., went on the search
for new businesses to acquire, it was, however, basically unknown
territory for the corporate management. A decade later, the situation has changed. Now telecommunications is one of the designat-
ed core businesses of Axel Johnson Inc. It includes two wholly
owned subsidiary companies, Hekimian Laboratories, Inc., and
Larscom Incorporated, which until 1993 was called Larse Corporation. (Though it is inaccurate from a historical perspective, the
company will be called Larscom all through this text).

Being part of Axel Johnson Inc. did not bring automatic benefits
to the telecommunications subsidiaries in the United States. As
mentioned in Chapter 12, there was neither any tradition nor experience in their area within the Johnson Group that they could
take advantage of. This made their situation different from the be-
ginnings of most of the other business units of Axel Johnson Inc.,
which as a rule started as offsprings of the Swedish Johnson Group,
using technology developed within the Group or drawing on the
experience of other Group companies. Neither of these was the case
with Hekimian and Larscom, a brief history of which this chapter
will provide. IDE – as mentioned in Chapter 12 – just put in a guest

appearance for two years without any success.

Hekimian and Larscom have a lot in common. Both were founded around 1970, both had early ties to the U.S. space industry, both are producing equipment for systems and services that help businesses exchange information electronically over telecommunications networks. When Hekimian was purchased in 1983, it was primarily on the grounds that it was a company of the right size and price with a promising future in a desired field. When Larscom was purchased four years later, it was primarily seen as a complement to Hekimian, a step in the corporate strategy to develop telecommunications into one of Axel Johnson Inc.'s main businesses. Initially, there were plans to integrate the two companies – at the start, the management of Larscom reported to the president of Hekimian – but these plans were soon revised. Larscom remained a direct subsidiary of Axel Johnson Inc.

The similarities between Hekimian and Larscom were not great enough to create synergies. Both companies produced equipment to monitor the quality of telephone lines, but their primary markets were quite different. Seventy percent of Hekimian's output went to the operators of public lines, primarily AT&T and, after 1984, its successors, the seven Regional Bell Operating Companies (RBOCs). Larscom's primary market was large commercial corporations that operated their own private telecommunications networks. Also, there were differences in corporate culture as well as location – Hekimian is located close to Washington D.C., while Larscom is situated in Silicon Valley in California – that made an integration of the companies cost more than it was worth.

Hekimian Labaratories, Inc., was founded by Norris C. Hekimian, an electronic engineer in whose living room the company's strategy was initially drawn up and whose cellar housed the early equipment

Dr. Norris Hekimian founded
Hekimian Laboratories in 1968.

prototypes. The other principals were John Kelly and Robert M.
(Bob) Ginnings, also electronic engineers. In the beginning, there
were some close contacts with NASA, the federal space program.
The first product from the new company was a manually controlled
phase jitter meter. The production ideas were there. The problem
was to raise capital; none of the owners had any funds to invest.
Thus progress was slow, but the modest ability to produce was
matched by a similarly modest demand.

A qualitative step was taken at the end of the 1970s, when
Hekimian moved from manually controlled instruments to systems. The »box business« – mobile instruments that had to be
brought to even the most remote installations – was replaced by
systems that from central locations could check a functionality even
in the periphery of networks.

In the middle of the 1970s, almost half of Hekimian's production
was exported to Europe. Later the domestic market came to mean
more and more, and in the 1980s, Hekimian was primarily dependent on U.S. customers, though some products were also distributed

Robert (Bob) Ginnings, an electronic engineer, joined Hekimian in 1971 and took over as president ten years later.

to Mexico and Canada. The company's main customer was AT&T. Bell Laboratories set the specifications for all equipment connected to its network.

In the early 1980s, the owners of Hekimian – foreseeing market and technological changes – realized that additional capital investment was required to support growth. Going public or selling the company to a financially stronger partner were the most viable solutions to obtain the capital needed. While either path would have allowed the owners to realize »the American Dream«, Norris Hekimian and his co-owners chose to sell the company. After talks with many companies over a two-year period, A. Johnson & Co., Inc., was introduced to Hekimian by Corporate Investors, a business broker from St. Louis. In June 1983, the company was purchased by Johnsons.

The first year as part of the new parent corporation was very profitable and Hekimian represented a substantial share of the total earnings of A. Johnson & Co., Inc. Soon, however, results declined. The breakup of AT&T in 1984 created an entirely new situation for

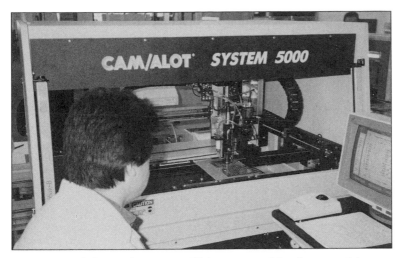

Computer-aided manufacturing at Hekimian provides the potential to produce short, specialized series with microscopic precision and high quality.

the whole American telecommunications business. The operation of the telephone network was no longer a monopoly. Instead, seven regional operating companies were created. It became more difficult for one actor to dominate both hard- and software production. The RBOCs were supposed to compete with each other, as well as with a number of other local exchange carriers. That created some problems and, at the same time, some new opportunities for Hekimian. Instead of directing marketing efforts towards Bell Laboratories, several independent companies had to be approached and there was no central authority to verify quality specifications. Competition became more open. At the same time, AT&T managed to cut Hekimian off from substantial parts of its old market to the benefit of the carrier's own »in-house« suppliers.

In addition to the market changes, in the middle of the 1980s there was also a technological shift, from primarily analog to predominantly digital transmission, that caused transitional trouble at Hekimian. A fairly substantial amount of new capital had to be invested, and the company was run at a loss for three years. In 1989, it was profitable again. Important market shares were resumed. The majority of the RBOCs used Hekimian's products, the most important of which was the REACT, a remote access and test system that lets users automatically test and monitor performance across an entire network.

While Hekimian saw the general network carriers as its primary customers, Larscom, at the time of Johnsons' acquisition, directed its efforts primarily towards private companies with their own networks, though they might also be using the public networks.

Larse Corporation was founded in 1970 by three engineers working together at Lockheed Corporation. One of them was George Larse, an MIT graduate of Norwegian descent, who gave his name to the company and became its first president. The company was situated in Palo Alto, in the midst of what had already become known as Silicon Valley, the famous concentration of electronics venture companies, many of which in some way or another were spinoffs from R&D efforts at Stanford University or the Lockheed space research center in the Bay Area.

During the first decade, the successful products were simple fire or burglar alarms. But the original concept at Larscom was to use large-scale circuit chips to produce equipment for transmitting a limited amount of data on regular telephone lines. A couple of years later, this equipment was used in remote monitoring and alarm systems, for example, to check fire or burglar alarms at industrial sites or detect faults in telecommunications systems. Potential customers were companies running power networks, pipelines, or AT&T (Pacific Telephone) with their microwave radio transmitting installations.

George Larse, whose great-grand-
father emigrated from Norway,
was employed as a researcher at
Lockheed when he decided to start
his own firm in 1971.

The Data-communicator was designed to combine signals from a
number of incoming lines, integrate and transmit them, check them
and, at the receiving end, separate them again. Later this equipment
would be combined in racks to increase the capacity of the installation. With the marketing of the system came installation and service
commitments. This line of production dominated during the late
1970s and early '80s, and made a fair amount of money.

The next step in the product development was to computerize
the system, allowing the user to create a data base showing station
names or functions and errors in plain language. An important contract was for the Alaska Pipeline, which required a fairly elaborate
system.

The AT&T breakup in 1984 opened new possibilites for Larscom.
In 1985, a new product was presented to the market that represented a first step in a new direction, high-speed digital termination. The channel service unit (CSU) could serve both as an interface
between private communication networks and the public telecommunication networks administered by AT&T, Bell or local opera-

In the telecommunications business, change is fast. The products from 1988 already seem dated. Larscom keeps up with the speed of technological development by continuously introducing new products.

tors, and as a means to monitor the performance of the communication systems. These units worked over an ordinary long distance line. They were later succeeded by data service units (DSUS) permitting work in high-speed communications. Network diagnostic systems were developed (TNDS) as well as different multiplexers (MUXS) and other access equipment that incorporated CSU and DSU functionality.

Lack of capital plagued Larscom from the start. Although the stock market was at the bottom in 1970, venture capital had to be found. Finally Rockcor, a Seattle corporation primarily doing defense-related research, acquired 49 percent of the stock and an option for a total acquisition. The financial situation also made it necessary to recruit employees who were willing to accept stock or stock options as important basic incentives.

In 1976, Rockcor bought the remaining stock of the company. In

1985, Rockcor was purchased by Olin Chemicals, a $2 billion corporation headquartered in Stamford, Connecticut. Larscom represented only a minor and foreign business to Olin and was soon put on the transfer list. A search for a new parent company started, ending up with Axel Johnson Inc. acquiring the company, the result of the common efforts of Priesing's special acquisition group and of Bob Ginnings, the president of Hekimian.

As mentioned earlier, the original plan was to consolidate Larscom with Hekimian. At first, the president of Larscom reported slightly reluctantly to Ginnings, but soon it was realized at the corporate level that no real synergy was accomplished by that arrangement. Soon after the Axel Johnson Inc. acquisition, George Larse was replaced as president by Mel Perkins, who was brought in, at Ginning's suggestion, to reorganize the company and find a new president. Responsibility for Larscom was subsequently shifted to the Axel Johnson Inc. chief executive. Perkins was succeeded by the sales manager, James Mongiello, in 1990.

By the end of the 1980s, the telecommunications business was once more profitable after some difficult years between 1986 and 1988. IDE, which never showed a profit during the years with Johnsons, was sold. Hekimian had overcome the troubles connected to the shifts in market and technology and again started to make money. The company had a superior technology for testing telecommunications systems, a strong market position in the United States and a strategy that included going international. Larscom, which had just been purchased, had shown a profit from the start and was at the beginning of a positive trend. Its products, focused on high-speed, single purpose termination, were in the technological forefront and already had a strong market position among the Fortune 500 companies.

Antonia Ax:son Johnson, here explaining her concept of »the good company«, personifies the modern businesswoman, and is also active in politics and social work.

CHAPTER FOURTEEN

Focusing and earning

Axel Johnson Inc., as the official name of the company has been since the beginning of 1988, was more profitable during the first years of the 1990s than during most of the preceeding decade. This was the result of work done by a number of actors.

Decision-making in business is often a long process characterized by formal and informal discussion, making it difficult to say exactly when this or that decision occurred. Formal decisions, recorded in the minutes of the board, are easy enough to pinpoint, but they are frequently just a confirmation of decisions that in reality grew out of dialogues between the chairman and the chief executive officer, among members of the board, among the company's officers or among people on the shop floor. As a rule, that kind of communication is oral and seldom results in written documents that can be used as source material for the historian, unless somebody makes specific notes or keeps an extensive diary. Therefore, what in the historic light seems to be the decision or the doing of one party may, in fact, have been the initiative of another. What the CEO pursues in terms of strategy often has its origin in the board's discussions or the owner's guidelines; likewise, the board members, and that includes the chairman, usually depend on the officers for the information that forms the basis for their decisions. Also, it is often desirable to design a decision-making process so that every party is involved and feels responsible; that very design makes it harder for the historian to distinguish individual contributions. In hindsight, therefore, it is often the chief executive officer who is visible and gets both credit for success and criticism for what went wrong. Of course, these comments are truisms, but they should be borne in mind when we discuss the process of change.

At Axel Johnson Inc., the configuration of actors looks as follows. There is the Board of Directors of the company, formulating the strategic vision. Foremost among the board members is, of course, the owner and chairman, Antonia Ax:son Johnson. A number of board members have been at her side over the years, each bringing her or his own personal and professional experience. In a special capacity, as »confidants«, Ernest Arbuckle and Vernon Anderson must be mentioned. Göran Ennerfelt, of course, also belongs to that category. Then there have been the presidents and CEOs: during the 1980s, John Priesing, who led the company in the first steps of its the strategic restructuring, and later his successors, Vernon Anderson and Paul Graf, who focused and developed the vigorous parts of the business, fixed or eliminated the losers and made the company a good generator of profits.

The change that Axel Johnson Inc. has undergone since the end of the 1980s can be described and analysed in a number of broad categories. There have been changes in scope and focus; in management, organization and owner-manager relationship; in performance measures and economic control; in geographic location; and in corporate culture.

John Priesing led the transition from dependence on oil earnings, for which he had been recruited, and introduced A. Johnson & Co., Inc., to the future-oriented telecommunications industry. During his period, the company still had the character of a conglomerate. Any subsidiary acquisition would, in principle, be acceptable as long as it was the right size and showed a proper earnings potential.

Vernon Anderson helped set the strategy that focused the company's resources on telecommunications and environmental technology – in which he oversaw an important acquisition – as engines for growth. Under this strategy, energy and materials handling would remain a stable and money-making business, and together the three groups would be regarded as Axel Johnson Inc.'s core businesses, to which the corporation could add value.

The most important task for Vernon Anderson – who accepted the appointment as president and CEO of Axel Johnson Inc. for a limited period of time only – was to find his successor. It took almost a full year, with the assistance of an executive search firm, before candidates could be presented to the owner. Antonia Ax:son Johnson's choice fell on Paul E. Graf, a 45-year-old engineer with experience in the electronics industry. Graf had spent a long period at Texas Instruments, including some years as general manager of its Brazilian subsidiary, then moved to Conrac Corporation, a diversified consumer electronics company where he reached the position of president in 1984 and CEO in 1986. Soon after, Conrac was purchased by another company and Graf went into the venture capital business as a partner of Schroeder Ventures. He took charge as CEO of Axel Johnson Inc. in October 1989. Vernon Anderson remained vice chairman of the board through 1992, and chaired the board's executive committee, with responsibility for long-term policy, through 1994.

Paul Graf's main objective, to use his own words, has been to create a business that is profitable for the owner. After 1989, a good working relationship evolved between the owner, the board and the president, where previous differences in scope, age and experience were evened out or turned into an asset. In addition to the frequent use of telefax messages, a routine of weekly telephone reports pro-

Paul Graf, president and CEO of Axel Johnson Inc. since 1989, an engineer with experience in, among other areas, the computer industry and the venture capital business, significantly increased the company's profitability.

vides the owner with the information that she needs in order to execute her function as chairman of the board.

On the basis of the board's discussions, Graf first turned his attention to the organization of the corporation in order to establish an efficient relationship between the head office and the business units. He made a clear division of responsibility: R&D, production and marketing are fully in the hands of the subsidiaries; corporate strategy, finance, and human resources development are mainly the concerns of the head office. Strategic planning has developed into a more regular routine and is now a management tool that appears a bit more formalized than before, but is also more sophisticated and reliable. The old personnel department was upgraded to a human resources department and a new manager was recruited. The objective was to take a more active approach to enhancing the competence and skills of all employees. The initial focus, in 1990, was on the development needs and career paths for women.

The corporate responsibility for finance, which implies that the head office represents the corporation in all its parts in the financial markets and functions as a bank vis-à-vis the subsidiaries, was not changed. A new main credit agreement was arrived at with a group of banks that offered the advantages of longer-term financing at short-term rates. Also, Graf changed the accounting principles, allocating the corporate debt, which previously was consolidated, to its origin at the unit level. In this way, he made the strong point that the president of each subsidiary was responsible for the overall economic performance of his unit, shifting the focus from revenues to return on invested capital. Thereby any false sense of profitability, which in some cases had been fostered, could be avoided.

Centralizing responsibility for finance and human resources did not mean that the head office would expand. On the contrary, in order to minimize corporate overhead costs, reorganization and

After 14 years at West 4th Street and 23 years at East 59th Street in Manhattan, the office moved to 300 Atlantic Street in Stamford, Connecticut.

cuts in the head office were called for. (The costs of administration at the subsidiary level were also regarded as too high; the business units were criticized for not being cost-efficient enough.) But there is a saying that stairs have to be cleaned from above; a hierarchial structure must be trimmed from the top down. It was quite obvious that cuts could and should be made at the corporate level. The size of the overall business just did not justify a head office of more than 20 to 25 people.

Moving the corporate head office from Manhattan to Stamford, Connecticut, provided an opportunity to adjust fairly easily the number of employees at the corporate level. Considerable savings in other areas were also possible: Calculations beforehand indicated that rent could be reduced by almost 70 percent. But the change of location was not motivated only by savings in rent or in the marginal numbers of persons who wouldn't follow. It provided a means – and this was not the least important reason – to escape the traditions that permeated the very walls of the New York office and to revamp the corporate culture. The move meant breaking with the old Johnson identification with oil, coal and steel that was so present in the dark, wood-panelled rooms at 110, East 59th Street, and adopting a more modern, light image in the new premises that were ultimately chosen in Connecticut. Also, in Stamford all personnel could be housed on the same floor instead of being spread over three floors, which would facilitate communication, another highly valued characteristic of Graf's corporate head office.

Modern management by objectives and decentralization of financial responsibility requires well-defined business measures to evaluate the performance of a company or a unit. In the strategic plans of Axel Johnson Inc., one set of measures is applicable to the corporate level while another primarily concerns the subsidiaries. To the corporate level belong guidelines concerning the size of the total business and the business units.

The first problem that needed to be solved was getting everybody to have a realistic view of the size of the company. With a majority of revenues coming from the petroleum wholesale business, there was a great deal of volatility as the result of rapidly shifting prices. Total revenue thus provided a poor performance measure and had to be given a much less prominent role. The focus shifted to non-petroleum revenue, and after several plan cycles – reflecting higher and maybe unrealistic ambitions – an interim goal of $300 million was established. Beginning in 1991, Graf began to show these revenue sources separately in both management reports and publications like the Company's annual report.

Some ratios concern earnings performance. Different principles have been used. Return on equity (ROE) is more adaptable to the corporate level than to the subsidiaries. In 1987, the ROE goal was 10 percent after tax, and in 1990 it was increased to 15 percent. As a comparison, the plan mentioned that the U.S. business average was about 11.5 percent ; an ROE of 15 percent would place the company in the top quartile of U.S. companies. These were substantial objectives given the corporation's average return on equity of about 2 to 3 percent in the 1980s. In 1992, the short-term objective was adjusted down to an average of 11.5 percent, while 15 percent remained as the long-term objective. In later plans, it was adjusted further downwards to 10 percent for the early 1990s and 12 percent for the latter part of the decade.

At the subsidiary level, return on invested capital (ROIC) was introduced as the performance measure; neither earnings (for reasons touched on above) nor ROE is appropriate. A whole set of ROIC goals were introduced with separate goals for each industry, taking into account the origin of the business. For example, an internally developed business such as Parkson was expected to do better than an acquired business that had much of the purchase price in goodwill on the books. ROIC goals ranged from 9 to 20 percent.

After significant debate, ROIC was abandoned for the energy business. A study of competitors revealed that the liquidity of the assets tended to allow high debt levels. The industry goal was not ROIC but ROE. In 1994, a goal called return on base capital was selected for the energy business. This mirrored ROE and could be easily applied to a subsidiary company. For non-petroleum-related businesses, Graf introduced profit before tax (PBT) as a performance measure, permitting an evaluation of results after the unit had

paid for the capital it employed. PBT became the primary performance measure for nearly all units for short-term review.

Another measure concerns the indebtness of the corporation. In
the 1987 plan, it was stated that long-term debt should be reduced
to 30 percent of total capital. Axel Johnson Inc. has always had a
higher total debt in relation to total capital, far from the 30 percent
objective. In later plans, the ratio is more vague; 30 to 40 percent is
mentioned, which per se is not noteworthy. The problem is that the
mix of a petroleum wholesale business and an industrial business
plays tricks on the ratio. Thirty percent is a good conservative ratio
for an industrial company, but the petroleum business, typically
more leveraged, needs to be included in a weighted average. Hence
the 30 to 40 percent range. Furthermore, the debt burden fluctu-
ates due to the seasonal variation in working capital, especially related to the oil trade with its unstable prices. In the long run, one of
the weaknesses of the company and a threat to its liberty of action
may lie in its dependence on banks and other creditors. The 1993
agreement with a group of financial institutions can be regarded as
a means of stabilizing the situation, since it included provisions
covering seasonal variations and fluctuations due to petroleum
price changes.

The strategic plans also comment on the dividend policy of Axel
Johnson Inc. As mentioned in Chapter 12, that policy had been discussed internally during the 1980s when dividends were sharply
increased for a couple of years. At that time, the dividend policy,
which was also a factor in agreements with creditor banks, was set
at 25 percent. Later, the company adopted a more flexible policy
with a considerably wider range so that dividends could reflect both
the company's business conditions and the owner's alternatives for
allocating capital.

In the strategic plans, there are also parts that comment on or set objectives concerning what could be viewed as corporate culture. This was touched upon in Chapter 12 as »the Johnson spirit«. The corporate culture of Axel Johnson Inc., as of other companies in the Johnson Group worldwide, consists of different elements.

First of all, Axel Johnson Inc. is a privately held company. The New York office clearly started, as we have seen, as a family business, in fact a private enterprise of the Consul General's. As that business has developed from a tiny office to a diversified corporation, the intimate family feeling has, of course, waned, but the principal status of being a private enterprise rather than a public company remains important. It defines the relationship between the company and its different stakeholders, stressing both the private company's obligation to uphold its integrity in relation to society and its traditional sense of responsibility vis-à-vis its employees and other stakeholders. An Axel Johnson Business Philosophy was adopted in 1988, stressing both »tradition and innovation« and calling for »a high level of business ethics and quality throughout the company« and a focus on »creating value for employees, the owner, customers and suppliers«.

Secondly, the owner and the president have been making efforts to establish the kind of climate that would lead employees to regard Axel Johnson as »a good company«. These efforts appear to have had some success. In 1994, a confidential survey of all employees was conducted by an outside consulting firm. More than 80 percent of the respondents agreed with the statement, »Overall, this is a good place to work«. According to the consulting firm, the average response for all U.S. manufacturing companies on this question is 65 percent.

The Business Philosophy also stresses the importance of recruiting »top talent« people and providing good incentive systems to motivate employees. At the same time, reflecting the private status of the company, it emphazises that Axel Johnson Inc. be »a family company with a family feeling«. A companywide newspaper, AxTimes, was started in the spring of 1989 to support human resources activities and to »emphasize openness of information and communication as well as encourage a family feeling within the company«.

The efforts to establish a good climate and to take good care of the company's human resources, in which Antonia Ax:son Johnson has taken a special interest, have also involved programs to enhance the careers of women in the company. The board has set the objective of having at least one woman executive at vice president level in each subsidiary before 1996. The fact that the owner is a woman has provided an impetus both to initiate and carry through these programs. In addition, the owner doubtless serves as a good role model for the female employees in her own companies, though there is still a long way to go.

By 1994, Karen Fraser, the new vice president for human resources, was working not only on the goal of moving more women into upper management but also on programs to develop all of the company's managers. These included a company-wide mentoring program and a specialized training program for younger managers. A company-wide job-posting program that made promotional opportunities available to everyone was also initiated.

The question of nationality can be regarded as a third element in the corporate culture. As we have seen, Axel Johnson Inc. started as an extension of the Swedish Johnson Group, and only after World War II, gradually evolved into more of a North American business. This altering of corporate identity was quite a normal process when the business logic was no longer determined by the makeup of the Swedish Johnson Group. In the 1987 strategic plan for Axel Johnson Inc., it was recognized that the time had come for the U.S. company to formulate a strategy of its own; until then, most strategic decisions had been made in Sweden. The very first point read as follows: »Build a North American Group of related industrial businesses.« A North American Group: There was no hint of any Swedish tradition or affiliation. It was also John Priesing's firm belief that the company would not gain any advantage from stressing its Swedish background, neither in the marketplace nor internally as a management tool.

The year after, Vernon Anderson reaffirmed the Swedish heritage in the identity of Axel Johnson Inc., but the company continued to be presented as a North American, independent company, sharing values with the other Axel Johnson companies and cooperating with them when advantageous, but holding its affairs »at arm's length«. In the future, the national identity of the company may become important as a consequence of its ambitions to operate globally, no longer as restricted to the domestic market as when it was primarily the U.S. operation of the worldwide Johnson Group.

The three core groups of businesses initially emerged as planned: Environmental and Industrial Products, Telecommunications, which had good growth potential both in terms of revenues and profits, and Energy and Materials Handling, which generated more cash than any other operation in the company. According to the 1988 strategic plan, each core business group would comprise at least three fairly homogeneous units of substantial size, with the two non-petroleum groups having revenues of approximately $150 million each. One manager would be responsible for each group, dividing his efforts between the corporate and business unit levels and reporting directly to the corporate president.

As it turned out, this plan was not entirely realistic, neither in

Enhancing the careers of women forms an essential part of the human
resource program of Axel Johnson, Inc. Here are the participants in the
first Women in Management Seminar, gathered in New York City in
December 1989.

terms of business growth nor of reporting relationships. By 1994,
there were four groups with the environment group being reported
separately from the industry group, plus the already mentioned
telecommunications and energy groups. While the focus had shifted to calling each of these »businesses«, the environment, telecommunications, and industry businesses each had two subsidiary units
reporting directly to Graf; these subsidiaries were not really that
synergistic.

Developing the core businesses required some acquisitions to
reach the desired size. No major purchases, however, were defined

in the strategic plans of the late 1980s. A couple of years later, when the business units had difficulties reaching their growth targets, it was clear that new production units, complementary in terms of technology, market or product mix, ought to be added to both Environmental Products and Telecommunications. It was not a question, though, of going back to the acquisition policy of the 1980s. Only small companies with above-average growth prospects were interesting candidates as new, free-standing subsidiaries. Vernon Anderson described this approach as a »seeds, not trees« strategy. ADS clearly met these criteria.

Graf introduced a second concept to accelerate growth. He refers to »bolt-on aquisitions« that could be fully and directly merged into an existing subsidiary, not to create another new business entity but to enlarge an existing one. Some of the minor purchases were of this kind, for example, the purchase of terminals for Sprague or the cases of T3 Technologies and Leybold Materials, discussed later in this chapter.

Focusing core businesses also meant divesting those units that did not fit the strategy, that did not meet the performance measures, or where Axel Johnson Inc. could not add value and contribute to a better performance. The divestment plans of the late 1980s were quite radical; the average consolidated invested capital should, according to the 1988 plan, be reduced by some 25 percent by 1990, making room for subsequent investment and growth in the core businesses. The strategy became less harsh in subsequent plans: A business that generated somewhat more than its capital costs should not be disposed of just for the sake of strategy unless it could be sold advantageously. It was necessary – that was part of the strategy – to make any divestment in the proper way, with due respect for the interests of the employees, and to find buyers who could offer the divested company a good fit. Furthermore, the owner was reluctant to take losses, causing a slower »fix and sell« approach to be followed. The sales of IDE (1988) and Aries (1989), of ITI (the Bearing Division was sold in 1990, the Ball Division at the end of 1993), the four cogeneration plants (1989–1994) and the Canadian divisons (Pennberthy in 1994 and Brian Controls in 1995) were all part of the strategic plan.

In Axel Johnson Inc., there has long been a fundamental belief in the strategic wisdom of investing in environmental technology, even if the return in the short term falls short of established performance measures. In recent years, this business strategy has been reinforced by the personal commitment of Antonia Ax:son Johnson to corporate environmental responsibility as reflected in the explicit environmental policy governing the Axel Johnson Group. An important acquisition was made in the environmental business.

In May 1989, an 80 percent stake was bought in *ADS Environmental Services Inc.*, an Alabama company that supplied flow monitoring equipment and services for municipal sewer systems. ADS was a rapidly growing family company, founded in 1975 by Peter Petroff, an electrical engineer and space scientist, and run by the founder and his sons Ralph, Alan and Mark, and Ralph's wife, Peggy Sammon. ADS had grown into the largest and most experienced company in the world in its market niche, measuring the depth and velocity of flows through underground sewer mains by means of computerized wastewater flow monitoring networks with telecommunication capacity. ADS had sales offices and service centers nationwide. The financial strength of Axel Johnson Inc. could help the company realize its growth potential, including an expansion into the international market.

In December of 1989, ADS bought an affiliate in Tennessee, *Southeast Environmental Services, Inc.* (SESI), that provided expertise

Son of the founder of ADS, Ralph Petroff is president of the family firm and leads it together with his brothers and his wife.

in the related inflow/infiltration reduction field. In 1991, ADS won a major contract in Australia, leading to the establishment in Sydney of Axel Johnson Inc.'s first totally controlled foreign operation. In the following years, ADS started penetrating Europe, where Germany, the United Kingdom, and France were the main target markets, though contracts were also secured in other countries. ADS also devoted considerable time and effort to R&D and training in order to develop its U.S. business. By the end of 1994, ADS had grown into a company slightly larger than Parkson.

The idea of purchasing ADS seems to have been Parks Souther's, who was hard pressed by the board to expand the environmental business. Originally the acquisition was regarded as a step in the direction of establishing an environmental group of businesses of the size that was mentioned in the corporate strategic plans. The president of ADS would report to the president of Parkson in about

ADS has found a profitable niche in providing automated flow monitoring systems for sewer mains.

the same way as the relationship between Larscom and Hekimian was originally envisioned. In neither case, however, was that hierarchical order maintained.

The Parkson business strategy had proved successful in the late 1980s, and the company continued to earn money in the early years of the 90s. 1992 was, however, a year of depressed earnings. Municipal funding declined, weakening the demand for Parkson's products, among which the Dynasand Filter had been the most profitable. The following year, 1993, business improved again. The future strategy of Parkson includes – and this has already started – going into the international market, primarily Mexico and South America. The search for new, complementary aquisitions for Parkson continues.

Telecommunications has, in the 1990s, developed into the most profitable business of Axel Johnson Inc. Earnings from operations

have greatly increased. Still this business would also benefit from a
third leg. It has not reached the »critical mass« as defined in the
corporate strategic plans. One obstacle is the very high price for
promising companies in the booming telecommunications sector.
Plans have been discussed to let some part of the company's telecommunications business go public in order to obtain the resources
to purchase the highly valued stock of a related business.

During the early 1990s, Hekimian developed into a winner. The
company is profitable, it has an advanced product and it has a solid
market base. Providing complete test systems is regarded as one of
Hekimian's competitive advantages. The company manufactures
and assembles the various units that make up its own systems and
can integrate other manufacturers' equipment when necessary. Customer education and round-the-clock service are part of the pack-
age.

The Regional Bell Operating Companies (RBOCs) represent
about 70 percent of Hekimian's market, primarily in the northern
and eastern parts of the United States. With five of the seven RBOCs
as customers, the company has quite a strong position in the U.S.
market. There has been considerable discussion about taking
Hekimian international, but so far, the return on investment of
North American projects has been sufficiently high to keep management's attention. However, the company's entry into the Mexican
market, beginning in 1985, has been very successful, and in 1991, a
sales office was opened in Hong Kong.

In 1990, Larscom acquired T3 Technologies, a small North Carolina company doing research, engineering and some production in
the field of high-speed communication. Its founders and owners
were Alan Mann, Jeffrey Ready and Dave Lollar. »T3« – a Bellcor
expression as was T1 – designates a cable permitting the transfer of
far more bits of data per unit of time than the common T1 cables.

Deborah (Debbie) Soon, educated at Stanford, Harvard and MIT, joined Larscom in 1990 as director of marketing. She became vice president of sales and marketing in 1993, and in 1994 she was appointed president of Larscom, the first woman head of an Axel Johnson Inc. subsidiary.

For a couple of years, there had been talks between Larscom and T3 Technologies about joint development work and marketing, and the result was the integration of T3 Technologies into Larscom. The T3 Division represents about 10 percent of the company's employees, revenues and profits.

The combination of telecommunications and computers has an especially promising future, creating a more intelligent product for the customer. »Connectivity« is the catchword. In order to highlight its new emphasis on the networking and internetworking market, Larscom updated its corporate image during 1993. This included a change of name – Larse became Larscom – which together with a more modern logotype and a new look indicated that it was in the communications business that the corporation saw its potential, going from single purpose, high-speed active termination equipment into flexible, multifunction systems for pro-active access solutions.

Larscom, where Deborah (Debbie) Soon, Axel Johnson Inc.'s first woman president, succeeded James Mongiello in 1994, is focused on developing and marketing high-speed broad-band products as well as service to both end-users – either the big telecommunications companies with common networks or big corporations with their own private networks – and service providers, who in recent years have established themselves as intermediaries in the market. The company already has a strong position in the U.S. market; however, unlike Hekimian, whose customers have an overwhelming majority of their operations in the United States, Larscom's customers are mostly multinational and want to use the same equipment throughout their worldwide networks – a challenge to the company's technical competence and culture. Agreements have been signed with distributors in the Pacific Rim.

In the early 1990s, the energy business increased its earnings from operations over the level of the late 1980s. Axel Johnson Energy Corp. is the responsible unit at the corporate level for oil supply and risk management; Sprague Energy is the distribution unit. During the early years of the 1990s, one third of Sprague's income came from heavy oils; one third from light oils, which was a remarkable expansion from the late 1980s; 25 percent from materials handling through the company's terminals; and 5 percent from other operations. The most important customers were the paper industry in New England, heating plants (which are often publicly owned), and oil retailers. In 1992, Sprague purchased Quinoil Industries, a wholesale heating oil business in Quincy, Massachusetts, and in 1994, a new terminal in Stamford, Connecticut. These purchases enlarged the company's network for distributing light oil.

Sprague and its affiliated companies' management and results were always kept separate from the failing cogeneration business; when combined into an overall energy category at the top level, the

Edward (Ned) Bulmer, trained as a marine engineer, joined Sprague in 1981. He rose through the ranks to become president of Sprague in 1986 and head of Axel Johnson Inc.'s energy business in 1992.

Peter Gwyn, president of Bird-Johnson since 1991, is leading the company into new naval and commercial markets.

performance of the cogeneration plants pulled down results. Divestment of the cogeneration operations had high priority and was completed in late 1994. Sprague is now a consolidated business with a good market position, primarily in the Northeast.

At Sprague, Henry Powers retired as president in 1986 and was succeeded by Edward (Ned) Bulmer. In 1992, he was given an added responsibility as president of Axel Johnson Energy Corp., where he succeeded Geoff Magrath. This is the only case where the plan to have one person in charge of an entire business area was carried out.

By the beginning of the 1990s, it was apparent that Bird-Johnson's strong concentration on the defense sector of the marine market was a potential Achilles' heel. Changes in the international balance of power signalled that it was time to plan for disarmament. Bird-Johnson's market seemed weak as a consequence of the breakdown of Soviet communism and the subsequent cutbacks in U.S. naval spending. Necessity demanded that Bird-Johnson pursue foreign navy ship programs and orient itself toward the commercial and non-Navy government sector of the domestic market. The company would produce propulsion equipment, not just propellers, for – among other uses – Coast Guard buoy tenders, fishing vessels, service vessels for drilling operations, tugs and other workboats. Also, it was indicated that Antonia Ax:son Johnson had always been uncomfortable with Bird-Johnson's position as a producer for the military sector and viewed it as somewhat alien to the ideas that she wanted to guide the Axel Johnson Group.

In the strategic plans of the late 1980s, the disposal of Bird-Johnson was mentioned. This would imply a profound change in the Axel Johnson identity in North America. The propeller business had been part of the company for so many years. This argument of tradition, which had also been mentioned in relation to the energy business, was not strong enough. Bird-Johnson was too small, and its growth prospects were unclear. The problem was to get »the right price«. After an unsuccessful attempt to sell the business in 1990, the company was taken off the market. A strategy of »fix-and-sell« was discussed and partly carried out; Bird-Johnson has been fixed and remains in the family.

The company, which in the early '80s had been very profitable, was doing poorly in the late 1980s and early 1990s. It was highly capitalized and did not provide the required ROIC. Even more capital was needed to keep up with modern technology. Production had to be made more efficient. In 1991, the new president Peter Gwyn took on that task. Gwyn had long experience in the marine industry and was, when recruited to Bird-Johnson, president of the Massa-

William Acton, who began his career with Johnsons at Ingersoll Johnson Steel Co. in 1979, was appointed president of Axel Johnson Metals Inc. in 1993.

chusetts Shipbuilders' Corporation. Before Gwyn's arrival, the company's Seattle foundry had been shut down and the facility continued as a repair and service workshop. Gwyn shut down still another foundry, in Mobile, Alabama, and consolidated all foundry operations in the Pascagoula, Mississippi, plant. The Mobile plant continued as a fixed pitch propeller repair facility. The business provided an acceptable ROIC in 1993 and 1994.

Over the years, there has been some ambiguity about whether Axel Johnson Metals, Inc. (AJMI), should be considered a core business or not. In the 1990s, it has – with the exception of 1991 – generated quite good revenues, but its long-term prospects have been unclear. A joint venture for producing silicon metal, Silarsa S.A., that was started in Argentina in the late 1980s with Axel Johnson Ore and Metals, an affiliated company, and an outside partner, had been a failure and was divested in 1994. Other ventures have been more sucessful. Since 1992, the second electron beam furnace in Morgantown has been managed as a joint venture with Titanium Metals Corporation (Timet). Timet has long been both an important customer and an important supplier for AJMI. The joint venture, called Titanium Hearth Technologies, or THT, is a separate company that was immediately profitable. By sharing furnace ownership with a customer, AJMI gained a reliable supply of raw material and a stable basic volume, balancing the typical swings of the industry. The joint venture can also be interpreted as a means of creating a variety of opportunities over the longer term, perhaps a step toward future integration both upstream and downstream for AJMI. In 1994, the company – run by William Acton, who succeeded Carlos Aguirre as president in 1993 – entered the nickel and superalloy markets by acquiring the assets of Leybold Materials, Inc., a small corporation in Vallejo, California.

»My most important task as president of Axel Johnson Inc.«, Paul Graf says, »is making money for the owner.« For private enterprise, profit is the essential objective. That is not to say that additional profits are always sought at any cost, regardless of other concerns, but it indicates the focus of management and the criterion of performance: the bottom line. Initially in this chapter, it was stated that Axel Johnson Inc. has been more profitable during the first part of the 1990s than during most of the 1980s. Here it remains to give some data to support that statement.

The table below shows a comparison between the periods 1980–1984, 1985–1989 and 1990–1994. For each period, average annual values are calculated for various financial measures. It must be borne in mind that the data presented for the subsidiaries just show earnings from operations. Because the cost of capital is not shown, the basis for comparisons between the different business groups is insufficient. It must also be noted that the telecommunications

Axel Johnson Inc.
Average earnings performance. Three five-year periods. ($1,000)

	1980–84	% chg	1985–89	% chg	1990–94
Operating earnings					
Environment	2,284	115	4,914	19	5,834
Telecommunications[1]	3,762	(160)	(2,270)	508	9,270
Energy[2]	5,445	(15)	4,614	88	8,682
Industry[3]	4,811	31	6,288	32	8,280
Subsid. earnings tot.	14,044	(4)	13,546	137	32,066
Corporate expense	5,883	15	6,790	6	7,202
Earnings from operations	8,161	(17)	6,756	268	24,864
Profit before tax[4]	8,407	(53)	3,922	382	18,906
Net income[4]	4,628	(33)	3,091	254	10,951
Shareholder's equity[4]	143,184	(4)	136,842	7	146,194
Return on Equity	3.2%	(28)	2.3%	226	7.5%

[1] 2-year average for 1980-84   [3] Includes numerous divested companies
[2] Includes cogeneration activities   [4] As reported

group was formed only in 1983, so the 1980–84 figure is actually only a two-year average. Also, other purchases and sales influence the data, but are not taken into consideration here. Nonetheless, some overall trends in the business development of Axel Johnson Inc. can be observed and discussed.

Looking first at the business group level, we see that earnings from the environment business have grown steadily. Parkson had a noteworthy increase in the early part of the 1980s, winning the »Company of the Year« award the first three times it was given. In the early 1990s, Parkson appears to have peaked as a result of the maturity of its markets, while ADS, which has achieved substantial growth in revenues, has not yet fulfilled its profit potential.

The telecommunications business was, as mentioned before, in trouble during the second part of 1980s but has recovered in a re-markable way, showing a substantial increase in earnings. In the last period, this group has the largest earnings, representing almost one-third of the total earnings of Axel Johnson Inc.

The energy business had a slight earnings decrease during the late 1980s, but average annual earnings increased again during the 1990s. The industry business, now consisting of Bird-Johnson and Axel Johnson Metals, has been performing well and steadily in-creased its average annual earnings by over 30 percent in both com-parisons.

Total subsidiary earnings were very similar during the first and the second part of the 1980s and increased by 137 percent in our third period. There was improvement across the board, but the largest increase came from the telecommunications business. Cor-porate general and administrative expenses seem to have increased during Graf's presidency in spite of the program to slim the corpor-ate staff. The annual rate of increase, though, was lower than during most of the 1980s.

The average annual earnings from operations are considerably better in the third period, an increase of more than 250 percent. The bottom line, net income, shows that average profits have been con-siderably larger during Graf's presidency than during the preceding period; they have also increased over 250 percent. That brings the annual average return on equity up to 7.5 percent. This is, it should be admitted, still far from the target ratio of 12 percent. But it must then be noted that the ROE for 1993 and 1994, the last years of our calculations, are 11.3 and 10.4 percent respectively. That suggests that the objective may not be that far away.

So, in the final analysis, we can conclude that Paul Graf and his staff has, in the short term, performed well and has substantially increased profits for the owner. Graf's strategy still has a bit of a conservative flavor; he emphasizes »making fewer mistakes«, perhaps because so much attention has been devoted to resolving the many problems that were reducing profitability in the late '80s. According to Graf, resolving these problems, redirecting a number of the individual subsidiary strategies, and improving the management system to insure that all subsidiary managers are responsible for their share of all costs have been the three most important reasons for the improved results of the 1990s. The five-year period ahead of us, 1995–1999, will present a significantly different challenge – making the company grow.

The Consul General was a farsighted businessman, but he could hardly
have foreseen the development of his New York office.

CHAPTER FIFTEEN

In essence …

So we conclude this story of Axel Johnson Inc. We have certainly not reached the final truth. History is continous interpretation. The historical image is always perceived from a specific angle. It differs depending on the position in time and space of the spectator and his or her values, interests and prejudices. As time goes by, the perspective changes and the interpretation alters, incessantly …

My focus has been on the growth of the company, the change in scope and strategy over time, and the relations between the American management and the Swedish owners. The long view has made it possible to see what technological change, especially in the development of the means of communication, has implied. We can also judge the impact of political and administrative decisions and institutions.

Roughly we can identify three main periods in the history of Axel Johnson Inc. We can name them after the leading actors. The first period, the Consul General/Wilkens period, was characterized by negative profitability, at least at the company level though not necessarily at the Group level. This leads us to look for other reasons for the owner's patience and the company's survival. During the second period, the Johnson Jr./Lynch period, the company started to earn money and was credited for it, but profits were uneven with some businesses providing very good yields and others drawn-out losses. The period since the beginning of the 1980s has been a time of restructuring, an endeavor that first affected profits negatively but cleared the ground for the gradual climb towards acceptable and good profit performance during the '90s.

Axel Johnson Inc. started modestly as a wartime makeshift, one-man enterprise established primarily to serve the needs of the Johnson fleet in the Western Hemisphere. The incorporation of the company in 1920 marked a difference in scope rather than in size. The shipping office developed into a trading firm, took on some new hands, representing additional competence, but remained a tiny organization. The strategy was changed. To sell and to buy for Avesta became the most important assignment. In addition to that, the orders were to do whatever business possible in order to defray the cost of the office. Later in the 1920s, oil purchases for Nynäs were added to the agenda.

At this time, the New York office was never an essential element in the overall strategy of the Johnson Group. Nevertheless, its business logic was decided almost entirely by the development of the Swedish operations. The office was not profitable until after World War II. Economic performance was not its raison d'être. That Johnsons persisted in having an office in New York must be seen in a light other than pure economic logic. It was widely acknowledged that the United States was the world's leading economy and the country of the future. It was therefore becoming, if not immediately rewarding, for a businessman of the Consul General's stature to have an office there, almost like an embassy. Once there, it was, of course, important that this outpost perform as well as possible.

With the younger Axel Ax:son Johnson, the mining engineer, came the appreciation of the American environment and the U.S. market as something different from the Swedish or European one.

The Consul General, Axel Ax:son Johnson, enjoyed his role as a country gentleman at Avesta. Here he is portrayed by Helmer MasOlle with his horse Sibylla and with the mill's chimneys in the background.

Partly because of personal circumstances, Mr. Johnson came to regard the New York company as an entity in its own right, representing specific business opportunities aside from the service it could render to the other companies of the Group. Still, much of what was done in the New York office was determined by the configuration of the Swedish Group. Gradually, however, the U.S firm was encouraged by the owner to develop a greater sense of independence. Both a reason for this and a consequence of it was the fact that the company became profitable, or showed profits. Now the operation started to grow and develop more diversified competence than before.

During the thirty years of Axel Ax:son Johnson's chairmanship and – most of the time – Robert M. Lynch's presidency, shipping and oil trading were the company's most profitable businesses. In the 1950s, shipping in its various forms provided a steady revenue when there was almost nothing else profitable in the company. Later, during the 1970s, the profit made in oil trading laid the foundation for the expansion of the next decade. The 1950s and '60s also saw the company enter new fields of activity – engineering and manufacturing. These enterprises still reflected the engineering competence of the Swedish Johnson Group. The transfer of Swedish technology to the United States played an important role in their development. From a Swedish perspective, the new activities can be seen primarily as an internationalization of Swedish business, exporting specific knowledge in naval construction, separation technology and metallurgy. Therefore, the new U.S. activities did not represent a higher degree of independence for the American affiliate, rather the contrary.

In the 1980s, more definite steps were taken towards a more independent status. The New York company should be – and here the old expression within the Group was used – a corporation »at arm's

Axel Ax:son Johnson Jr. spent his formative years in the United States, realized what it took to succeed in the American market and transformed the New York trading office into a diversified, manufacturing U.S. corporation. One of his great interests was horses, and he started breeding American Morgan horses in Sweden.

length« from the Swedish Group. This change had to do with two separate chains of events. First, the restructuring of the company, reducing the dependence on oil and investing in telecommunications and environmental technology, meant moving in a direction where the Swedish Group had never been. Second, the Swedish Group was so thoroughly restructured itself that there was no basis for the old kind of ties any more. In fact, the sole remaining tie was the common owner, Antonia Ax:son Johnson. The question of the American company's »Swedishness« had been reduced from an actual technological and economic dependence to a potential ingredient in the corporate culture.

The growing independence, which was part of the owner's business strategy, can also be regarded as the coming to maturity of the U.S. company. The signs of a new internationalization of the business are especially interesting in that light. What started with a bridge from Sweden to the United States has now formed a platform from which new bridges are thrown across the world. Somewhere among these small endeavors – in Australia, in different European countries or along the Pacific Rim – the viable nucleus for the Johnson Group of the 21st century may hide.

During the first thirty years that the American company existed, the Johnson Group was highly centralized and the owner a patriarch, exercising all the prerogatives that belonged to his position. The Consul General's ambition to control the New York office was as strong as his wish to control the offices in Gothenburg or Malmö, but his actual ability to supervise details was highly limited due to the distance and the available means of communication. With his international experience derived from the European scene, it seems as if the Consul General did not fully realize the distinctive features of the U.S. market. Communication between the Group headquar-

Antonia Ax:son Johnson has developed the American industrial company
that she inherited into a modern, focused and profitable enterprise. She
also inherited her father's interest in horses, here Rubber Duck.

ters in Sweden and the office in New York was either by mail, which was comprehensive but slow, or by telegram, which made possible a rapid but scanty exchange of orders and reports. The combination of strong centralization and hampered communication created a climate of uncertainity and mistrust that did not foster the creative spirit of entrepreneurship necessary for entering the American market. Nor did the accounting principles used during the interwar years reflect the actual flow of affairs or the performance of the American business.

The period that followed was characterized by quite a different relationship between the owner/chairman and the president of the company. Certainly, Axel Ax:son Johnson assumed a position as patriarchal as his father's in the Group, but his relations with the top management of the U.S. company were much more intimate. In a way, he had grown up in the company and in American society. He frequently spent time in the United States and participated in business decisions much more actively than his father had been able to. The expanding means of communication facilitated this new role. Regular flights over the Atlantic Ocean also made it possible for the president of the American company to appear often in Stockholm. Telephone calls to a great degree replaced both telegram and mail as tools for managerial exchanges. In the historical perspective, Johnson and Lynch appear on the American business stage as a couple, each with his part to play, complementing the other and developing a deep friendship that also included their wives. A strong feeling of »family« embracing key executives and their families on both sides of the Atlantic Ocean is reflected in the sources.

In this respect also, the 1980s meant the dawn of a new age in the New York company. The intimate feeling was swept away and the new generation leading the company established a more profes-

The board of Axel Johnson Inc. evolved in the 1980s from a formality into an arena for the formulation of business strategy. Here the 1994 team, from the left, William I. M. Turner, Jean Allard, Göran Ennerfelt, Antonia Ax:son Johnson, Paul Graf, Lawrence Milligan and Vernon Anderson.

sional relationship, the design of which was a source of dispute, ultimately leading to the shift of president from Priesing to Anderson and later to Graf. The owner gradually assumed a more logical, or modern, role, using the company's Board of Directors, not the executive group, as her arena of action.

In earlier years, the board of Axel Johnson Inc. did not play an important role, sitting in the shadow of the patriarch. The exception was during the period of Axel Ax:son Johnson's illness, when the board, and especially Ernest Arbuckle was active. During the 1980s, the board became both the arena and the vehicle of change. The most important owner initiative was the change of president and the reformulation of strategy of the late 1980s. Today the daily details of the business are no longer the owner's concern, which in the historical perspective appears slightly ironic: When communication technology most effectively bridges the geographic distance, the »arm's-length« is rigorously kept, not only between Axel Johnson Inc. and the rest of the Johnson Group, but also between president and owner, in due respect for their different professional roles.

The turning points in the history of Axel Johnson Inc. are quite easily identified and can, with the risk of being repetitive, be stated thus: the establishment of the New York office during the first World War, the incorporation in 1920, the increased independence of the late 1940s, the beginning of production in the United States in the 1950s, the entry into the oil trade in the 1960s, and the restructuring during the 1980s, which implied entering new areas of business characterized by the modern features of high technology in combination with worldwide service. We see in these events the effect of strategic decisions by the owners, the board and the presidents of the company. But the evolution is also, and that is the point here, the result of changing political conditions to which the business actors adapted. With this perspective, we can see the decision to etablish an office in New York as a reaction to the shipping situation created by naval warfare, especially the German strategy of unlimited submarine assaults and the British and American quest for control over neutral shipping in the Atlantic. The incorporation of the company was a natural adaption to current legal practice once it was decided to maintain the office in peacetime.

The new strategy of the 1940s and 50s – making the company profitable and starting production in the United States – was primarily motivated by changes in Swedish legislation in two areas, currency regulations and inheritance taxation, which made it worthwhile to earn dollars both to strengthen the Johnson Group's international liquidity and to build up an independent company outside Sweden as a future financial safeguard for the family.

Going into more extensive oil trading was a decision taken basically on business grounds, securing supply for Nynäs. But the reason why this business became so profitable can be found in the political situation. In the 1970s, two oil crises created unforeseen market conditions that, in combination with clever use of the U.S. energy legislation, resulted in profits never before heard of in the history of A. Johnson & Co., Inc. The restructuring of the company in the early 1980s was, likewise, an adaption to changing markets but also to the political situation, namely the abolition of federal support to the independent oil companies. New lines of business had to be found.

It is tempting, as a conclusion, to reflect a little on what has constituted the »Johnsonness« of the Axel Johnson Group. From where we are now, and with the perspective we have, the wheel seems to have come full circle. Johnsons started, in Sweden as well as in the United States though at different points of time, with trade and service. The business concept called for a flexible form of operation with no heavy investments that tied up capital in specific geographic regions or industry sectors. It implied making profits out of floating process, not out of rigid structure, and that certainly requires a specific talent. Around the turn of the century, Swedish society was industrialized and so was the Johnson Group. Fixed assets were purchased in order to produce tangible hardware using an industrial logic. After a time lag, the New York company also swung into traditional industry. In our days, both society, globally, and business are leaving the industrial phase of development and heading towards something new that in important respects re-sembles preindustrial business logic. The most important assets are no longer fixed investments like buildings or machinery but the in-dividual knowledge of people and the collective competence of the organization, the techical know-how, the research orientation, the market connections and other intangible resources of the company.

The restructuring of Axel Johnson Inc. can be interpreted as an adaption to, or rather, a way of participating in this new phase of business development. The flexible character of business, the focus on process, is coming back. The direction of both the telecommuni-cations and the environment businesses towards flow control – whether electronic data or water – and service and education in con-junction with that, is significant. Profits are made by using expertise and taking creative advantage of ongoing industrial and societal flows and processes. This comes close to the old tradesman's ideal of being flexible, keenly alive to the possibilities presented by continous change. And tradesmen they have always been, and they put their pride in being, the Johnsons.

References

The sources for this story are both archival and oral. The historic material of the entire Johnson Group is stored in the central archives in Engelsberg, Sweden, whence the core of the older Axel Johnson Inc. material has also been transferred. In Engelsberg are the company's annual reports, the auditing reports, the correspondence between the presidents and the owners over time, and various dossiers on different subjects. A general reference is made to these series of documents. In the following notes, every letter that has been used as a source will not be referenced unless directly quoted or for some other reason. I have kept a version of the text with complete references.

Recent material is stored in archival warehouses in the United States or at the corporate headquarters of Axel Johnson Inc. in Stamford, Connecticut. Recent material concerning the company's business units is filed at their respective premises.

In addition to the written sources, I have interviewed a number of people. In many cases, it is quite obvious what their contributions are. With some people, I have had a series of talks intertwined in the writing process. Some of them have commented on different versions of the text. Especially in the description of recent history, their views have been a prominent source. That is the case with Antonia Ax:son Johnson, Göran Ennerfelt, Paul Graf and Robert Lynch, and to some extent, Vernon Anderson. Also, Pauline Bilsky has influenced my opinions on the chain of events.

From a scholarly standpoint, this situation is not without risks. These persons are all, in different capacities, actors in the story, and they have, as we all have, an interest in seeing and remembering certain things, disregarding and forgetting others, fitting the past into the logic of the present. On the other hand, this is the kind of challenge that the contemporary historian must cope with. It is up to the reader to judge whether I have managed to balance the story properly. What I am talking about is, of course, the question of objectivity as a scientific norm. Is it possible to uphold objectivity in a commissioned business history? Personal feelings and current business interests necessarily influence the description of the most recent events, when, as is the case here, the story is brought up to date. Lack of historic perspective must be weighed against the wish to inform about the latest developments.

In addition to those already mentioned, the following persons have contributed to this book through interviews or discussions: William Acton, Carlos Aguirre, Bo Ax:son Johnson, Ursula Burger, Irving Brown, Edward Bulmer, Walter Busch, William Dunham, George Gebauer, Bob Ginnings, Peter Grace, Carl-Evert Gustafsson, Howard Harker, George Larse, Elisabeth Macias, Geoffrey Magrath, Charles Orem, Henry Powers, John Priesing, Lennart Rehnquist, Donald Ridley, Richard Sandquist, Debbie Soon and Parks Souther. A number of other people have been helpful and informative while showing me around, or participating in lunches and dinners during my visits to the different business units. Joseph Smorada, Charles Seitz and William Ball have provided information for the appendices.

CHAPTER 2: Incorporation

PAGE 15
The early development of A. Johnson & Co in Sweden is analyzed in Holze, Bengt (1973): *Axel Johnson och A. Johnson & Co. 1873–1890.*

PAGE 13
The history of AB Separator and Lavalco is described in Gårdlund, Torsten and Fritz, Martin (1983): *Ett världsföretag växer fram* I–II: *Alfa Laval* 100 *år*. L.M. Ericsson's American venture is analyzed by Jan Kuuse: »En koncern växer fram«, in Attman, Artur et al. (1976): *L.M. Ericsson* 100 *år. Pionjärtid, kamp och koncessioner, kris* 1876–1932. About Swedish

investment in South America, see Runblom, Harald (1971): *Svenska företag i Latinamerika. Ekonomiska mönster och förhandlingstaktik.* Scandinavian University Books.

PAGE 21

About W.R. Grace's history, see the article in Derdak, Thomas (ed; 1988): *International Directory of Company Histories*, St. James Press, Chicago and London, and Clayton, Lawrence A. (1985): *W.R. Grace & Co., The Formative Years* 1850–1930, Jameson Books, Ottawa, Ill. The collaboration with Johnsons is not, however, mentioned in these books.

PAGE 27

Much of the narration here builds on the correspondence between Ekström and the Consul General.

Ekström's ambitions for the future are described as completely unrealistic in a biography on the Consul General: Högberg, Staffan (1990): *Generalkonsuln*, Norstedts, p. 105.

PAGE 28

Quotation from a letter from Johnson to Ekström, 09/17/19.
Benckert's letter to Johnson is dated 03/30/19.

PAGE 31

About the Detention case, see the paper by Lennart Forss: *The Detention Case*, undated, Axel Johnson Inc. archives, Engelsberg. This long drawn-out affair, in which Ekström's services were used even after 1923, was later negotiated at the government level and finally concluded in the 1930s.

CHAPTER 3: Selling steel for Avesta

For this chapter, the correspondence between Johnson and Wilkens is the main source of information.

PAGE 35

About the new start, see a letter from Johnson to Ekström, March 1923.

PAGE 37

Quotation from a letter from Johnson to Wilkens, 04/09/23.

PAGE 38
Quotation from a letter from Johnson to Wilkens, 05/14/26.

PAGE 41
About Swedish iron exports to the United States, see Attman, Artur (1986): *Svenskt järn och stål* 1800–1914, Jernkontorets Bergshistoriska skriftserie nr 21, p. 41. On the steel crisis, see Pettersson, Jan-Erik (1988): *Från kris till kris. Den svenska stålindustrins omvandling under* 1920 *och* 1970-*talen.* On the history of the Fagersta Works, see Söderlund, Ernst – Wretblad, P E (1957): *Fagerstabrukens historia. Nittonhundratalet.* On Sandviken, see Carlsson, Sune: »Ett halvsekels affärer«, in Hedin, Göran (ed; 1937): *Ett svenskt järnverk. Sandviken* 1862–1937.

PAGE 42
On Harding's role, see also Högberg (1990), pp. 164–166.

PAGE 44
Quotation from a letter from Johnson to the New York company, 02/04/24.

PAGE 48
Quotation from a letter from Johnson to the New York company, 07/28/25.

PAGE 52
Quotations from a letter from Wilkens to Johnson, 02/16/29, and Wilkens to Johnson, 04/22/29.

PAGE 54
On the status of the stainless licenses, see Högberg (1990), p. 194.

CHAPTER 4: Buying oil for Nynäs

PAGE 56
Quotation from a letter from Johnson to Ekström, 07/02/21.

PAGE 57
About the Swedish oil consortium, see Runblom (1971), p. 171.

PAGE 68
Quotation from a letter from Gunnars to Wilkens, 08/14/31.

PAGE 69
Quotation from a letter from Hedström to Wilkens, 11/28/34.

PAGE 70
About Swedish oil imports during World War II according to the Swedish Oil Investigation Committee, see SOU 1947:14: *Handeln med olja,* table 1.

CHAPTER 5: Communication, competence and confidence

PAGE 79
The argument about Swedish investments in the United States is taken from Ågren, Lars (1990): *Swedish Direct Investments in the U.S.,* Institute of International Business, Stockholm School of Economics, pp. 212–213.

PAGE 81
Quotation from a letter from Johnson to Wilkens, 03/12/25.

PAGE 82
About the Consul General's scepticism, see Högberg (1990), p. 172.

PAGE 83
Quotation from a letter from Johnson to Wilkens, 04/03/25.

It is not clear if Dudley Dupignac was related to a Frank Dupignac, also a corporation lawyer, who played a not entirely honorable role in Lavalco at the turn of the century, see Gårdlund (1983), pp. 176–178.

PAGES 85–86
The telegrams and letter are dated 01/12/27.

PAGE 89
On Högfelt's mission, see the transcript in a letter from Högfelt to Johnson, 11/05/41.

PAGE 93
Quotation from a letter from Wilkens to Johnson, 10/08/45.

CHAPTER 6: The new role

PAGE 95
On Högfelts intention, see a letter from Johnson Jr. to the Consul General, 05/08/47.

PAGE 96
On Kinzel's experience, see the memo of 05/15/47.

PAGE 100
Quotations from a letter from Kinzel to Johnson, 12/01/50, and from Johnson Jr. to Lynch, 04/29/53.

PAGE 101
On the Swedish currency regulation, see Wihlborg, Claes: »Valutapolitiken« (The currency policy) in Werin, Lars (ed, 1993): *Från räntereglering till inflationsnorm.* SNS förlag, Stockholm.
For information confirming that the problem persisted for the Johnson Group for several years, see the letter from Johnson Jr. to the Consul General, 02/01/52.

CHAPTER 7: Shipping

In this chapter and Chapters 8–12, I have made extensive use of the annual reports for the years 1953 on, as well as the auditing reports from Price Waterhouse. I have also used information gathered during long interviews with Lynch. Lynch has kept unique source material in his diaries and in a series of »problem sheets« – memos that he wrote according to a specific formula on different subjects, often as a preparation for his presentations and discussions with the owner. These were put at my disposal at a late stage in writing this history; I have only been able to make partial use them. There is also an undated document by Lennart Forss, a longtime employee of A. Johnson & Co., Inc., with responsibility for the iron powder business: *A. Johnson & Co., Inc., A chronological catalogue of events…*, that has provided useful hypotheses. In this chapter, I have also used information from Walter Busch.

PAGE 108
On the Amtorg traffic, there is a variety of source material in the Axel Johnson Inc. archives in Sweden, like draft of contracts and letters exchanged with Soviet as well as Swedish authorities.
Quotation from a letter from Johnson to Wilkens, 05/10/40.
Concerning the effect of the Amtorg charters on later relations with the Soviet authorities, I rely here on an interview with Lennart Rehnquist, who for decades was responsible at A. Johnson & Co HAB for the business in the Russian market.

PAGE 109
On the Liberty ships and the Panamanian companies there is a late memo in the archives by Forss, to which Lynch has added his written comments.

CHAPTER 8: Naval technology

Not much source material can be found in the Bird-Johnson archives in South Walpole, Massachusetts. Unfortunately, a large portion of the files was discarded in the mid-80s due to lack of space. In this chapter, I rely heavily on the annual reports of A. Johnson & Co., Inc., on interviews and memos provided by Orem and Ridley, and interviews with Lynch. Basic information on the product line is found in Bird-Johnson Corp., delivery list »Controllable Pitch propellers«.

PAGE 134
Quotation from a letter from Ridley to the author, 07/08/92.

CHAPTER 9: Oil

In this chapter, apart from the interviews indicated above, I have also used information from Priesing.
Furthermore, I used a memo in the company's archives, J.C. Johnson: *History of the consolidated oil division*. Mimeograph, 1977, and a document titled *Inc consolidated oil division long range plan*, 1979–1984.

PAGE 143
Sprague's early history is described in Powers, Henry M. (1985): *C.H. Sprague & Son Company – A New England Colossus*. The Newcomen Society of the United States.

PAGE 145
For a general history of oil and energy politics worldwide, see Yergin, Daniel (1991): *The Prize. The Epic Quest for Oil, Money and Power*. Simon & Schuster, New York.

PAGE 152
The different opinions on the rationale behind the purchase of tankers come from interviews with Lynch and Ennerfelt, respectively.

CHAPTER 10: Environmental technology

In this chapter, I have drawn on a short interview with C. E. Gustafsson and longer interviews with Souther, who has also provided written material for my use.

PAGE 162
Quotation from a memo by Lynch, 08/31/70.

PAGE 163
Details from the Lamella purchase are taken from C. E. Gustafsson: *Parkson Corporation, Monthly report, June* 1971. The agreement included Parkson's obligation to send periodic reports to the Institute. I have used some of them, e.g., *Parkson Corporation, Quarterly Report: Exploitation of the Lamella Products, July* 1971 *through March* 1972.

PAGE 165
Information on the 1973 strategy is taken from a letter from Gustafsson to Lynch, 09/12/73.

PAGE 166
On the six-month respite, see a letter from Souther to Priesing, 03/27/86.

The 1980 strategy is presented in *Parkson Corporation, Presentation to the Board of Directors of A. Johnson & Co., Inc., April 9th,* 1980, added to a letter from Lynch to Souther, 12/22/80.

PAGE 168
Quotation from a letter from Souther to Priesing, 03/27/86.

CHAPTER 11: Machines and metals

PAGE 170
The story of Kamyr is based on a memo by Knut Dahl, the Norwegian president of Kamyr, Inc., dated 07/20/51, and on a letter from Björkman to Johnson Jr., 02/14/52.

Quotation from a letter from Johnson Jr. to Dormsjö, 06/19/50.

PAGE 175
Information on the Ingersoll purchase, the motives behind it, and the situation in the mill is also drawn from *American Metal Market*, 15 *June* 1976, and from local papers.

CHAPTER 12: Restructuring

In this chapter I made extensive use of information from Antonia Ax:son Johnson, Ennerfelt, Lynch and Priesing.

PAGE 189
For the story of NCC, see Larsson, Sören & Saving, Jaak (1990): *Nordstjernan inifrån*. Norstedts.

CHAPTER 13: Telecommunications

In this chapter I have, in addition to sources mentioned earlier also used information from Ginnings, Soon, Macias and Burger.

CHAPTER 14: Focusing and earning

In this chapter, aside from other already mentioned sources, I have relied heavily on the Axel Johnson Inc.'s: strategic plans, on the company newsletter, *AxTimes*, and on written and oral source material from Graf and Anderson.

Appendix 1

A. Johnson & Co., Inc.
Profits/loss 1920–1947. ($1,000)
Source: Annual reports.

Year	Profit (loss)	Year	Profit (loss)
1920	3	1934	(5)
1921	(12)	1935	(2)
1922	(2)	1936	(11)
1923	(10)	1937	(20)
1924	(19)	1938	(12)
1925	(27)	1939	(12)
1926	(19)	1940	41
1927	(36)	1941	2
1928	(16)	1942	1
1929	(4)	1943	(1)
1930	(5)	1944	3
1931	(14)	1945	1
1932	(13)	1946	19
1933	(7)	1947	18

Note: The high profit in 1940 was largely due to the income from the Vladivostok shipping operation.

TABLE 2

Axel Johnson, Inc.

Net income, dividends and stockholder's equity (S.e.),

1948–1993. ($1,000). Source: Annual reports

Common stock, included in stockholders equity, was 1948–1951 $200,

from 1952 on $370. No dividends are recorded prior to 1977.

Year	Net income	Dividends	S.e.	Remarks
1948	3		76	
1949	(101)		(26)	Fall in commissions
1950	4		5	Refund of federal taxes
1951	46		51	
1952	19		240	
1953	7		247	
1954	22		269	
1955	41		308	
1956	23		331	
1957	40		859	
1958	5		375	
1959	53		428	
1960	64		492	
1961	47		539	
1962	32		571	
1963	114		685	
1964	57		719	
			756	Adjustment to balance
1965	80		836	
1966	94		930	
1967	102		1,032	
1968	107		1,139	
1969	392		1,531	
1970	102		1,633	
1971	878		2,511	
1972	2,292		4,803	
1973	14,866		19,669	Oil crisis!

Year	Net income	Dividends	S.e.	Remarks
1974	16,089		35,758	
			53,702	Adjustment to balance
1975	9,613		63,315	
1976	4,893		68,208	
1977	346	74	68,480	Heavy losses at Ingersoll
1978	338	74	68,744	Heavy losses at Ingersoll
1979	61 424	111	130,057	Oil trade!
			129,725	Adjustment to balance
1980	8,318	555	137,488	
1981	10,594	555	147,527	
1982	4,163	555	151,135	
1983	(7,438)	555	143,142	Recession
1984	7,502	555	150,089	
			139,093	Adjustment to balance
1985	8,338	0	147,072	
1986	(4,736)	830	141,578	Hekimian's bad year
1987	2,110	11,100	133,235	
1988	2,400	9,455	126,678	
1989	7,341	600	133,398	
1990	397	1,805	132,768	
1991	8,571	99	141,314	
1992	13,080	6,847	146,168	
1993	16,506	3,270	159,015	
1994	16,203	10,000	164,595	

Appendix 2

A. Johnson & Co., Inc./Axel Johnson Inc.
Board of Directors 1920–1994

Gustaf E. Ekström	1920–1923
Edward G. Robinette	1920–1923
Ernst E. Rosengren	1920–1923
Leo W. Wilkens	1923–1946
Stoddard B. Colby	1923–1930
Curt H.T. Benckert	1923–1930
Dudley Dupignac	1925–1926
Vilhelm Björkman	1930–1949
George J. Kraft	1930–1946
Andreas Högfelt	1946–1947
Charles S. Haight	1946–1948
Robert K. Kinzel	1947–1953
Bernard T. Atwood	1949–1950
Axel Ax:son Johnson, Jr.	1951–1988
Honorary chairman	1984–1988
C. Harold Björnander	1951–1966
Robert M. Lynch	1953–1989

Walter S. Busch	1955–1981
Ernst C. Arbuckle	1963–1986
Stig A.R.Sultan	1966–1981
John A. Walstrom	1968–1979
Paul E. Owens	1968–1974
Christer Agell	1968–1969
Norris Darrell, Sr.	1968–1979
Director emeritus	1979–1980
John S. Russel, Jr.	1975–1988
Arthur W. Hawk	1975–1981
Antonia Ax:son Johnson	1978–
P. Göran Ennerfelt	1978–
John W. Priesing	1978–1988
J. Bertram Ladd	1979–1994
Director emeritus	1994–
William I.M.Turner	1986–
Vernon R. Anderson	1986–
Jean Allard	1987–1995
Paul E. Graf	1989–
Lawrence D. Milligan	1992–

Index of persons

Photographic credits

Many photographs in this book are from the archives of the Johnson Group in Sweden or the United States. We have been able to trace the origin of the photographs on the following pages.

The author

The author, Hans De Geer, has since 1995 been responsible for establishing a Center for Ethics and Economics at the Stockholm School of Economics. He received his Ph.D. in history in 1978. He has specialized in contemporary history and written a number of books and articles on themes such as scientific management, computerization of society, industrial relations and business values. From 1991 to 1994 he was professor of business and work life history at the School of Business, Stockholm University. He is currently working on a comprehensive history of Axel Johnson AB.

EHF   Institutet för ekonomisk-historisk
        forskning vid Handelshögskolan i Stockholm
        Institute for Research in Economic History,
        at the Stockholm School of Economics

Previously published in the Institute's series:

GÖRAN B. NILSSON   *Banker i brytningstid.*
                     A. O. Wallenberg i svensk bankpolitik
                     1850–1856. (1981)

JAN GLETE   *ASEA under 100 år, 1883–1983.*
                     En studie i ett storföretags organisatoriska
                     tekniska och ekonomiska utveckling. (1983)

TOSTEN GÅRDLUND   *Ett världsföretag växer fram.*
                     Alfa-Laval 100 år.
                     Del I. Förhistoria och uppbyggnad. (1983)

MARTIN FRITZ   *Ett världsföretag växer fram.*
                     Alfa-Laval 100 år.
                     Del II. Konsolidering och expansion. (1983)

GÖRAN B. NILSSON   *André Oscar Wallenberg*
                     1. Odysséernas år 1816–1856. (1984)

JAN GLETE   *Storföretag i starkström.* (1984)

ULF OLSSON   *Bank, familj och företagande.*
                     Stockholms Enskilda Bank 1946–1971.
                     (1986)

JAN GLETE   *Ägande och industriell omvandling.*
                     (SNS Förlag 1987)

HÅKAN LINDGREN — *Bank, investmentbolag, bankirfirma.* Stockholms Enskilda Bank 1824–1945. (1987)

MARTIN FRITZ — *Svensk stålindustri under efterkrigstiden.* Internationell konkurrens – marknader – försäljning. (1988)

JAN-ERIK PETTERSSON — *Från kris till kris.* Den svenska stålindustrins omvandling under 1920- och 1970-talen. (1988)

ERIK DAHMÉN (huvudred.) — *Upplåning och utveckling.* Riksgäldskontoret 1789–1989. (1989)

GÖRAN B. NILSSON — *André Oscar Wallenberg.* II. Gyllene tider. 1856–1866. (1989)

ULF OLSSON (red.) — *Aspekter på FFV.* (1993)

SVEN GERENTZ — *Individer, familjer och block.* Köpmän och köpenskap på Gotland 1894–1994. (1994)

HANS DE GEER — *Axel Johnson Inc.* 1920–1995 (1995)